Short Stories

SHORT STORIES

——BY——

KYRLE BELLEW

Privately Printed by
THE SHAKESPEARE PRESS,
114-116 East 28th Street,
New York.
1912.

PREFACE.

New York City, Sept. 1st, 1911.

My Dear Frank:—

You, who know me best, accept this little book. I dedicate it to you. Shakespeare calls me an "abstract and brief chronicle of the time." Marie Corelli says I am only a "Monkey." Dead or alive, "Some one has blundered" in Stratford.

Many estimable persons in the calling I use to get my living, and a few profound critics of matters relative to that calling, declare their admiration of me for "My kindness to my relations," but deplore my inability to sustain my title to any professional aptitude whatever, whilst other equally estimable persons and critics in and out of my calling, declare I am "Great."

So I am in a quandary how to nominate myself. Accept me then as my Mother brought me into the World—and as the World knows me—plain Kyrle Bellew—and your Friend.

I have been many things, amongst others, a Sailor, an Australian Station-hand, a Gold miner, a Cattle drover, a Grave digger, an Explorer, a Book-keeper, a Journalist, a Dramatic Critic (God forgive me) an Author of many fugitive contributions to various and varied periodicals; have perpetrated a few successful plays, and a few others. Have wandered the World over; done all the unwise things men do; repented of many of them; shall live I hope to repent of many more. Have not any claim to the veracity of George Washington or the equally unconventional attributes of St. Anthony. Good, bad, and indifferent labels have been ticketed throughout the world upon the back of my character and I stand as a kind of Sign-

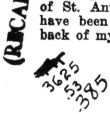

post to many whom I know, and heaps whom I don't, warning them from those paths of dalliance which I have trod, sometimes choked with thorns, have so often been strewn with roses; and from which I could always at least admire another, which they told me I should have trod. A path along which my eyes were never blinded to any wayfarer and along which it has been a joy to see you so steadfastly trudge.

Friend: This chamber is pleasant where we have often sat, surrounded by trophies that mark the milestones of my life. Neither you, nor I, can look round its walls, or into its cabinets, or on its book-shelves without recalling incidents that are dear, some sacred to us. Among those oft told, a few have served to interest our intimates by the telling; and in thought of the joy of your companionship as the tales were told, I have jotted down a few of them here, that perhaps some day, somewhere, when I am gone, they may remind you of the laborer who has rejoiced and suffered, lost and won, by your side, and whose greatest happiness in life, is to be sufficiently worthy in your eyes to exchange with you in all trueness and sincerity that holiest, most sacred name on Earth: The name of *"Friend."*

KYRLE BELLEW.

FORE-WORD.

Dear Reader: There is a tradition amongst Australians that three classes of story-tellers exist—Liars, D— —d liars, and Mining Experts.

There are also three kinds of fools: Plain Fools, D— —d fools, and "New Chums."

I have been a Mining Expert, and every kind of fool, including the New Chum. Now I have fairly warned you.

If you care to read farther through these pages you will find both my confessions verified.

Fiction is greater than fact—because, one has to invent fiction, and fact just happens without your being obliged to bother about it.

"In medias tutissimus ibis." With this proverbial philosophy in my mind, I have steered the middle course between the two.

There are many people in the corners of the Earth to which Fate has led me, should this volume ever fall into their hands, who will recognize the incidents herein set down and the occasions of their occurrence. They will probably content themselves with classing me somewhere in the category ending with "Mining Experts."

Every reader I feel confident will put me down a fool, perhaps a D— —d fool or worse. It is my privilege to forestall all, and accept the situation, you see, as gracefully as I can, contenting myself with the satisfaction of a conscience cleared by the confession of my shortcomings.

If it amuses you, dear reader, to say with the immortal Rosalind, "These are all lies"—Say it and be happy. If, on the other hand, it contents you to believe these sketches, "Mainly about Myself," are true, —you will do yourself "no harm" and me "no wrong."

I pretend to no literary excellence or style. In these pages I talk to you in the language of men on the quarter-deck, in the reporter's room, 'round the camp-fire, in the bush, in the theatre and in everyday life.

My i's are not dotted nor my t's crossed any more than they would be were I recounting these stories viva voca. Such niceties are the attributes of fiction rather than fact. But if I have helped in these pages, to lighten the dullness of even a minute of your time, I shall have done well, and so I leave you to go ahead and read my book, or not, just as you please.

CONTENTS.

SHORT STORIES
by KYRLE BELLEW

MAINLY ABOUT MYSELF.

My beloved mother told me I was born one Thursday morning early, unfashionably and uncomfortably early; on the 28th of March. The year of Grace of my advent, which I have no means to verify, has been put down in almanacs and newspaper records anywhere between 1845 and 1860. As my dear father did not happen to be married until 1848-49, and I was the youngest but one of a moderately numerous family, the former date suggests a situation which happily, no less an authority than Ulster King-at-arms contradicts; the latter date I know to be wrong—unhappily! My nurse, bless her heart, when to this day, I remember with the tenderest feelings of undying affection, always impressed upon me the legend that I was "found in a band-box under a cabbage." Dear, deceitful soul—rest in peace!

So, you see, even in my earliest childhood, my mind was sorely puzzled to discriminate between fiction and fact. I must say, the picture I conjured of myself, wrapped in beautiful clean tissue-paper, tied up with a lovely pink ribbon, or possibly a blue one, reclining in a pure white band-box under the shade of a dew besprinkled cabbage, was intensely alluring.

I never could settle in my mind why the cabbage was selected by "Willie," my nurse, and I ventured to question the genus of the plant that sheltered my discovery.

But in spite of suggestions from me of "bulrushes," "rose bushes," and other more decorative plants, Miss Wilson stuck to the cabbage. Failing to shake her adherance to the succulent vegetable, I let it go at that. I never see a cabbage growing, however, even to-day, but the difference between us arises in my mind; and were "Willie" once more to revisit the earth, I feel, if we met, I should still try to induce her to reconsider the matter of the plant, under whose shade I was introduced to the world.

The troublous times of the Indian Mutiny gave me my first impressions of life. Of these I have only vague recollections; and I am not sure to-day, whether those vivid pictures, that come back to me out of the mist of the past, are not the memories of my parents transmitted to me in early childhood.

I know we were up in the hills of Chirapoongee, and came down to Calcutta, passing through many perils. In those days there were no railways, and I remember being borne along in a kind of chair, held by a broad band passed around the forehead of a stalwart native bearer. I remember days spent in a howdah on the back of an elephant. I recount many days and nights on board a pinnace; it was a green pinnace—green and white, floating along down the silent waters of a broad river. I can to-day see again large fires along the banks lighting up the darkness of the Indian night, with a lurid glare as we drifted along. I can hear yelling men and see them dressed as soldiers—and can recall the frequent firing of guns—and wondering why "Willie" used to make us lie down flat on the floor of the vessel's cabin, while my mother and she cowered down over us and sobbed.

I remember my father and mother kissing us all good-by, as we left the ghat with "Willie" in a native dinghy, and were taken alongside a large ship, lying out in the stream off Prinseps Ghat, Calcutta.

My next impressions are of the sea. I do not remember missing my father and mother—Willie to my eyes the most beautiful thing on earth was with us—and we children of the "Padre Sahib" in Calcutta Cathedral were the pets of the ship, and that same Captain Toynbee, whose name is dear to every man that sailed in those days, and for many a long year after from the port of London.

I could write page upon page about the great East Indianmen of the past, but as my life, save for this one voyage as a little child, had nothing to do with them I will refrain. I suppose that from my early associations with it, and perhaps because my mother was the daughter of a distinguished Admiral, I gained my first and my undying love for the sea. It has called to me all my life, and it calls to me as strongly to-day, as it did in my youth. Above all things the sea has ever been mistress of my heart. I can remember too, seeing my first steam engine. It was at Plymouth when the long voyage was over, and we were taken ashore.

Then all was wonderment. England where everything was so green—where everyone was white—where we had no ayahs, no bearers—no palkees and nothing we were used to. We were installed in a little house in St. John's Wood. I remember it well. The whole place would have gone into the hall of the lovely home in Harrington Street, Calcutta. We were not happy. It was so gloomy and cold when the winter came. I remember the snow—and above all I recollect my dreadful chilblains! Then things happened, we didn't understand.

Strange people came; at last father arrived—and he came alone. Years followed. We moved to a pretty little home near his grand big church; a tutor came to take care of us boys; the girls went to a school, and "Willie," our beautiful and well-beloved Willie disappeared. A turning point seemed to come in all our lives, when one day my father told us we were going into the country for the Summer, and on the platform of the Waterloo Station, a very handsome and beautifully dressed lady come up to us and we were told she was our new "mamma."

That day set the first period in my life—and I can feel now the consternation the revelation of this new order of things created in my small breast. I adored my father. I was jealous of his love. I felt I had suffered a bitter wrong—I didn't know why. Something went out of my life, and something came into it that left me dazed. I grew in an instant into a rebel, and a great desire filled me to get away from home.

We went to the Isle of Wight, and in the delight of that beautiful summer spent in the most picturesque spot behind St. Katherine's point, I temporarily forgot my troubles and revelled again in the contemplation of the glorious sea and the frequently passing ships, whose white sails dotted the lovely sunlit water of the Channel.

The French fleet visited Portsmouth, and my dear father, who was persona grata with all the great folks, took me one day on board the flag-ship of the Channel Fleet, at that time, the two-decked wooden line-of-battle-ship "Edgar." We lunched aboard and then visited the "Victory," and spent the rest of the day in the dock yard and amongst the men-of-war. A new world opened to my eyes, and I made up my mind there was only one thing in it for me—and that was a life at sea.

I brooded over the matter and at last told my father, who opposed the idea as I was his only boy left, my elder brother having gone into the world under the aegis of Mr. Henry, the great railroad magnate of America. I was unhappy at home; I never got on well with my new "mamma," and at last one day I ran away, determined to go to sea.

I had a few shillings in my pocket, and away I went, wending my way down the river to the Great East India docks at Blackwell. Lying in the Export dock nearly ready for sea was a large Indianman, on board of which I stole. The riggers were aloft bending sails; and, in the bright sunshine the life and color—the salt water smells of tarry ropes and new canvas—intoxicated and fascinated me.

I wandered about the ship unheeded—watched the cargo lowered down the hatches and lastly forced by an irresistible longing to go aft—clambered into the port fore-rigging and crawled up the first two or three ratlines above the sheer pole.

Some one sprung beneath me, and before I knew what had happened, I found my feet seized with rope yarns to the shrouds, and a voice sung out—"Now, Young 'un, you'll have to pay your footing."

What was meant by this very rude person, clad in a tarry jumper and a pair of very dirty overalls, I hadn't the least idea. I felt uncomfortable, and my uneasiness increased on seeing the mate coming forward with a grin on his face, calling out "Come down out of that, youngster! What are you doing up there?"

He had me cast adrift, and I gave all the money I had to the man who lashed me up, on his explaining to me that any one not belonging to the ship, venturing aloft had to "pay their footing"—in other words stand drinks to the men.

The mate called me aft and began to question me, discovering among other things my name and who I was.

"Want to go to sea, do you? Well, you take my advice, youngster. Go back home as quickly as you can, and if you must go to sea get your father to send you—and don't try running away any more. If you don't promise me—I'll tie you up to a stanchion till knock-off time, and then, damn me! I'll take you back myself."

My father, being so prominent and well-known all over England, the mate knew that he would have done quite the right thing for himself in acting as he threatened.

I promised him, however, to return home at once, and I left the docks with a sad heart, but more determined than ever to go to sea.

Next day was a terror. My father had been making all sorts of search for me, as I did not get home until four in the morning, having walked all the way from the docks.

I arrived tired out—dirty and hungry.

I shall never forget my dear old dad in his night shirt opening the door. He simply said "Go to your room. I'll talk to you to-morrow."

That to-morrow!

I told him the truth—got a hiding for running away—but with it such a salve as I never hoped for, in his promise to let me go to sea.

I didn't care for anything on earth. I didn't feel the hurt when I sat down in silence and disgrace at breakfast. I was completely, ecstatically happy, and in a few weeks found myself alongside the gangway of H. M. S. Conway, with my cadet's kit in my regulation chest, with my name in big letters painted across the front, and my uniform on in which I felt as if I owned the earth Poor dear old dad! A tear rolled down his cheek as he kissed me and said: "God bless you, boy—I wanted you at home with me."

Well, I went to sea,—and years after I left it. I travelled the world over. I became a gold-miner in Australia, a newspaper man, reporter, editor, even a dramatic critic—out in that great country. I wandered about as a stockman, a station hand, everything a man can be in the bush. I saw life in every phase, until at last chance brought me to the stage. There let me stop. Some of the incidents of my life I have jotted down in the following pages.

As I look back on them I live again in the past, and out of my dreams came the faces of many I have loved, and who have believed that the foolishness and adventures of my life have not been without some good—even if only to serve as a kind of moral finger-post to others which way not to go.

If my "good fairy" ever visited me again and gave me my "wish," it would be to meet some kind-hearted old millionaire, who would give me a big sailing ship, and send me off to roam about the world at sea, and so "live happy ever after."

SOCKS

Summertime. Place: On board H. M. S. Conway lying in the Stoyne. The ship was dressed from flying jib-boom to taffrail with many-colored flags. Her yards were manned and, as the guns of the guard-ship, H. M. S. Donegal, thundered out a royal salute, His Royal Highness, the Duke of Edinburgh, stepped over our gangway and we all cheered ourselves hoarse.

It was a great day! The Mayor and Corporation of Liverpool, all the great shipping magnates, with their wives, daughters, "sisters, cousins and aunts," and many of the parents of cadets belonging to the ship, were on board to witness the drill, inspection and annual distribution of prizes by the Duke—also the performance of a play, prepared by us after many weeks of anxious rehearsal, in which I was cast for the leading lady. I was to be one Laura, I think it was, in "Time Tries All."

Why I was chosen for such a prominent part, I am at loss to conceive unless because as a youngster I was possessed of a somewhat gentle manner and a face that lent itself to the requisites for making up to look like a girl.

A great big fair-haired, good-natured fellow named Cummings (he died of cholera, poor chap! in Bombay and we buried him the same evening down at Colaba), Bobby Knowles, whom I have never seen since, and Fred Passow, who after many years of service in the navy accepted a fine appointment with the Inman Line, and now commands one of their magnificent steamers, are the only others of the cast that I can now recall.

Bobby Knowles had to be one of my lovers. I remember that there was a scene where he knelt at my feet. And I think Fred Passow was the inevitable "other man." There was also an episode with poor Cummings, but what it was has faded from my memory.

The main deck aft on the starboard side served as our stage and was gracefully draped with flags. Our audience sat on rows of chairs and forms arranged the same way as when we "rigged church" on Sundays. His Royal Highness and suite were in the middle of the front row surrounded by the Mayor and Corporation and the officers of the ship. Behind them were the distinguished guests and in the "gallery" or at the back of all, the couple of hundred cadets and the ship's company.

For some reason I was a prime favorite with the Captain's wife, and she had volunteered to provide the necessary dresses for my part. I had to appear in a riding habit and over this arose my first difficulty. We couldn't "fake" a riding habit and couldn't go to the expense of having one made. However, a very pretty girl—the sister of one of the boys—a strapping, rosy cheeked, healthy-looking English girl of about eighteen came to our rescue. She lived at Rock Ferry, off of which we were moored, and often came aboard to visit her brother. She would "lend her own riding habit for the occasion." That solved one difficulty, but when I came to put it on, the fact that she measured in every direction except up in the air about twice as much as I did was at once apparent. Something had to be done—but what?

Passow suggested towels.

Knowles roared at the sight of me.

Cummings voted, "Stuff him with socks."

Poor Mrs. Moull took me into the Captain's room, and after pondering the matter, decided there was nothing for it but to follow Cumming's suggestion.

Our respective chests were at once ransacked and
all the available socks brought up to complete my figure.

We had a regulation method of folding our socks,
making each pair up into little ball. When my toilet
was completed, I looked a bit bubbly and lumpy, but
we smoothed things down as much as we could and
every one said it looked fine. "It," I presume, being
my figure.

Dear Mrs. Moull beamed on me with delight. Captain Moull grinned over over his good-natured, old
face. But Cummings and Passow mortified me to
blushes by making side-remarks about my figure,
which they compared with everything unlike the vir-
gin beauty I was supposed to represent.

The prizes were given, the Queen's Gold Medal
awarded, the Duke's speech vociferously applauded, inspection and drill were over, and, while the visitors
were being "regaled" at a repast, the shrill pipes of
the boatswains' mates blew the call, "Rig Church!"

My heart began to beat fast. The long prepared
for, but awful moment had arrived. We all got ready
for our parts. The audience was seated. The band
played and finally the curtain rose on, "Time Tries
All."

Our audience was delightfully cordial. The Duke
laughed good-humoredly and all went swimmingly until Bobby Knowles knelt at my feet and began his
love scene. I think I had to "scorn him." Anyway,
whatever it was, I had to rise from my chair and with
an indignant gesture bide him "Begone!" It was something of that sort.

I did rise. I did throw out my arm. I did all we
had rehearsed, but, in doing it by some means or other,
my bosom unbuttoned and out came a pair of socks,
which fell to the deck and rolled along to the feet
of the Duke.

Some devilish shipmate at the back sang out,

"Bravo, socks!"

The Duke roared—and so did every one else. I lost my head and could hear nothing but the jeers and yells of delight from the two hundred or more young devils in the "gallery." At length, stung to desperation, I tore open my bosom, and seizing the rest of my "figure," threw the socks like so many cannon balls at the heads of my tormentors. There was an uproar. Back came the socks. Amidst a scene of uproarious laughter and confusion, the curtain fell upon my first appearance on any stage.

We all got a horrible wigging from the Captain, but His Royal Highness was perfectly delighted, and voted that the amusement he had derived from our escapade was far beyond what he anticipated, and begged Captain Moull to pass the matter over. The Duke looked up aloft as we manned yards when he left the ship and he was still laughing when he got into the barge that pulled him away.

Some years afterwards, His Royal Highness visited India in the H. M. S. Galatea, of which ship Fred Passow was one of the junior officers. My ship was in Bombay, and I was in charge of the boat our ship sent ashore to the Apollo Bunder, where the Duke embarked to report himself on board the "Forte" frigate, then carrying the Commodore's flag at the station.

There were boats from each of the various ships in the harbor. All the crews tossed oars as the Prince came down the bunder, and we stood up in the stern sheets and saluted as he passed along.

Suddenly he stopped opposite my boat and a broad grin lit up his features. "Haven't I seen you somewhere before, youngster?" he asked.

I saluted and answered, "Yes, sir."

"Where was it?"

"On the Conway, sir."

"Socks, by God! I thought so!" cried the Prince and passed on roaring with laughter.

A REAL GHOST

"Yes, I have seen a ghost—once," I said in answer to an inquiry while my company was standing round the stove of a wayside station waiting to connect with a train bound east from St. Paul.

"After I left sea, I went out gold mining to Australia—made money, failed—and at last found myself installed second mate of a large English clipper full of passengers and bound for London. We cleared away from Sandridge pier about mid-day, and our last passenger to come on board, was a young fellow in a long brown ulster—ulsters were new then and remarkable. The only other one I knew was worn by Fanny ————, a beautiful young girl who had lately arrived from England and to whom I had become greatly attached.

"The passenger was shipped home by his friends with special instructions to our captain to keep him away from liquor. He was an absolute wreck from drink. Our booby hatch had been filled at the last with a quantity of colonial wine, one of the first shipments home from the colonier; but there was plenty of room in the cut of the hatchway for a man to stand.

"Well, we had been to sea some weeks, and were battering away 'round the Horn with a head wind and cold as the deuce. The snow and ice were thick everywhere, and it was blowing hard. I swore if I once got out of it I would never voluntarily go to sea again. One night I had the middle watch, that is from twelve to four in the morning, and I was sitting on a hencoop under the weather cloth in the mizzen rigging, when I heard the captain come up. He had with him the young man in the brown ulster. The captain gave me orders; took a turn up and down, said good night, and went below.

"There was no one left on the poop but myself and the man at the wheel, for it was so cold I gave the youngster who had to strike the bells, leave to go below until I called.

"I suppose I must have got numbed by the cold and slept, for I was awakened by the relief wheel, at four bells, who gave me the course as he went below. I took a turn aft and saw the young man with the brown ulster leaning over the taffrail; but when I turned aft again he had gone down the companion, which faced the helmsman, and was the only entrance on deck from the saloon.

"I asked the helmsman how long the young man had been on deck. I was somewhat taken back when he assured me there had been no one there. I thought I had been dreaming, so did not press the matter.

"Shortly afterward the moon, which had been obscured through the clouds and made everything—covered as it was with snow—bright as day. As I turned aft in my walk I saw the man in the ulster leaning over the lee rail close to the helm. I walked aft to speak to him. As I approached he turned toward me in the moonlight, and to my horror I saw the face of Fanny ————. The figure stood for a moment and then seemed to go overboard.

"I shouted out 'Down with the helm! Man overboard!'"

"The watch came tumbing aft. In a moment all hands were on deck. The ship flew up the wind and I swung her main-yard aback.

" 'Who is it, Mr. Bellew?' asked the Captain.

" 'The passenger, sir,' I answered, 'with the long ulster.' We lowered a boat, but there was no trace of him. The muster-roll was called and the young fellow was gone sure enough.

"We braced up our yards and filled away again, and after a few days ran into fine weather and forgot all about the lost passenger, who was duly entered in the log book as lost overboard.

"One day in the tropics the captain gave orders to have the hatches off and let some air into the hold. The last hatch to be removed was the booby hatch aft, an ornamental teakwood affair on which passengers used to sit, and which formed quite a feature of the quarter-deck. As we raised the hatches a peculiarly sickening smell came up from the hold.

" 'There's dead rats there, sir, sure,' said the carpenter to me.

"Off came the hatches, and there, to our horror, in the fierce sunlight of the tropics, with everything bright and gay about us—children laughing and playing, every one happy—we disclosed the bloated and decomposed corpse of the young man in the brown ulster. By his side was a broken case of wine, and two or three empty bottles, showing plainly how he had died.

"The problem of how he got into the hold was soon solved. There was a large brass ventilator just abaft the main fife-rail, and knowing that drink was stowed down there he had lowered himself down to get it.

"On my arrival in the Thames our long-looked-for mail was brought on board by our agents. Among the first letters I opened was one bearing the Melbourne post-mark. I opened it hurriedly, for I was anxious for news. It was from a stranger, simply inclosing a newspaper paragraph:

" 'On Sunday last at No.— ——— Street, East Melbourne, Fanny, only daughter of Thomas ———, Esq., died, of inflammation of the lungs.'

"My mind rushed back to the night off Cape Horn when I had seen her face in the moonlight. I turned the leaves of the log-book and there, on the same date as the notice in the newspaper clipping was the entry: 'Richard ————, passenger; jumped or fell overboard, 3 A. M., signed, 'KYRLE BELLEW, Second Officer, Ship T—— S——.' ''

POOR DEVIL

"Ah! old man. That's it; that's just it! What did I do it for? Hanged if I know; because I was a born fool I suppose. Did I care for her? Is it me? Not I, faith—at least—no. You see it was this way, Harry. Ah, but the year's too long—an—you're nearest the billy, old man, slue yourself round and lift it off. So—"

It was Christmas Eve. Not the long chill-nighted eve of jolly old England, but hot—blazig hot, and up on the reefs at Solferino, away to the north of the Clarence river, New South Wales.

We were up there amongst the first of the rush. Gold! But the times were bad now, the wages low.

Jack and I were mates. He'd been at sea; so had I. Met at the store and mated over Laird's rum—warranted. Egad, it wanted some passport down a fellow's throat, for the drays hadn't been up for over a month; and I'll swear there wasn't a sign of old Jamaica three weeks before, at the long weather-board shanty that did duty for everything in the shape of civilization on the reefs. Jack wasn't half a bad sort, frank, free—and twenty-three. We mated.

It seems years ago. The first time I saw him, was with a swag over his shoulder, an unmistakable serge shirt on his back, a thatch of his head that a "Conway" boy would have revelled in, jerked jauntily back with the peak at "full cock;" a six-shooter stuck in his belt, and altogether looking about as jolly and new-chumish as any fellow who had yet come up to the rush.

Work was over for the day, and there were eight thousand of us—of all nations and all colours—lounging about the camp. The store was in our centre—

Jimmy Laird's "claim" we used to call it—and, by
Jove, it was the richest claim on the whole diggings.

The boys hailed Jack with a shout. He just stopped for a moment, and the collie trotting beside him
settled into a long, low growl.

"Shut up, Kaiser," and then he walked into the
thick of us.

He was too free and jolly not to take all hearts,
and before he'd settled down amongst us an hour, his
voice was ringing through the place in a rattling song,
and he'd made a dozen friends.

"Where'll I camp at all to-night, I wonder!"

I offered him a corner in my hut, and he came.
That's how we met. He shouted rum—and then we
went down the creek together—and never parted
again on Solferino.

We built our humpy down in a quiet nook away
from the camp, pegged out a claim on the "Don Juan"
line, and worked it, till the lead ran out and times got
hard. Ours was a strange, wild life, with a lot of ups
and downs—chiefly downs; but we got on well together, and were happy.

Christmas Eve! We'd just came from the store—
been laying in a stock for the next day.

Christmas Eve, with a cloudless, clear night, and a
grand moon. Our iron bark fire crackled cheerfully,
the cool air just lifting up the smoke which, as it rose,
mixed with the long branches of the trees above. We
didn't feel like turning in, so stretched out upon the
grass, and set to thinking.

Kaiser cruised round a bit, but soon settled; and
turning his wistful eyes first at one and then at the
other of us, snugged his nose down between his paws
and went to sleep.

I was thinking of home away in England, wondering what they were doing there. Next day an empty
chair would be placed at the table in my old place,
and a dear voice, I was destined never to hear again,

would say, "God bless my boy, and absent friends."

"Say, old man," said Jack after a bit, "did you know I was married?"

"You—good God!—no."

"Begorra, then, it's a fact."

"Where's your wife?"

"Devil a bit of me knows. Somewhere South, I think."

"You think! Scissors, man, if I'd a wife—I'm thinking, I'd know."

"Yes—happen you would," and his hand wandered towards Kaiser.

A log of wood, burnt through in the middle, fell in two upon the fire, sending up a cloud of smoke and sparks.

"Curse the smoke!" and turning away his head for a moment, Jack wiped his eyes with the rough sleeve of his shirt.

"If you don't know where she is, old man," I said, "what did you do it for?"

It was at this point Jack spoke the opening sentences of this story.

I handed him the billy, and lifting off the lid, he took a drink of the stuff inside; we called it tea.

I knew, if I waited, he'd tell me all the story, for we were true mated, and his bothers were mine, as much as mine were his. He took a pipe from the leather pouch on his belt and filled it. Getting it fairly alight he lay along with his face to the fire, and began.

"Harry, old man, it's often a smiling face that hides a sick heart—mine does. What did I do it for? Well, it was this way you see. I was a born fool—from the first—darned if I wasn't a fool for being born; but that wasn't a matter of choice with me—if it had been, expect I'd have done something else more foolish.

"My poor old governor—God bless him!—brought me up for the army. Of course, I ran counter, and chose the sea. Well, I went to sea; gay old times I had of it, too, till they wanted me to stop at home. I stopped, and the governor thought he'd make a respectable member of society of me.

"He put me in an office—shipping firm in Leadenhall Street. It was something—something—and Co. I forget what now. Anyway I cheeked the 'Co.' first day I was there; kicked a coon out of the office, the second for cheeking me, and the third, I flung a directory at the head clerk for calling me a 'useless article.'

"I left next day. Coming down the street soon after, I saw the 'True Briton' stuck up outside Wigram's office, to sail for Melbourne.

"That's how I got here, Harry.

"Ever in Melbourne? No! Oh, well, it's a fine kind of place. I thought it would be paved with gold, but it wasn't. It was blue stone, and jolly hard to find a soft berth on. Well, old man, there was a doctor's daughter—and—oh, you can imagine the rest!

"She cared for me a bit, I think, and I think I cared for her. I think I—but there—that's all gone now. Yes, I did love her, old man, loved her with all my heart.

"She went away to Adelaide on a visit, and I did not hear from her. A fellow came up from there a week or two after—a fellow I knew—spoke about her —said she was flirting with another man. I wish I'd crammed the dirty lie down his throat, but I didn't. I was a born fool, and took it to heart—nursed it up till it grew big and filled every fibre on my body.

"Damn it! it was a rough one on me. I don't quite know even no what I did. I used to cruise round, and then—well—I forgot—drink, I think.

"One night I was in the theatre, and two ladies, one an old, the other a young one, came and sat in a box behind me. They talked French. I'd seen them there often before. The younger one was an actress. They were there again next night, so was I. Same again next. It was raining. I got them a cab.

"Then I called—fool!——Yes."

He paused for a bit, and flicked the ashes out of his pipe.

"Harry, old man, I spooned that woman—I don't know why. She wasn't pretty—at least—no—she wasn't; fine eyes, that's all—but still a kind of face you'd have to turn round and look at twice.

"I used to buy her little presents. She liked the rings I wore. I gave them to her, all but one—a plain broad gold band, with a 'love of a life,' engraved on it in old English letters. She wanted that too—but I couldn't get it off. She got it off, though and looked at it—asked me what the writing was. I laughed and told her, though I felt as if a knife had gone through me. The ring had never left my hand since—since—well, since the girl I'd cared for, put it there and kissed me, under the trees by the gate—at her home. —Heaven! Harry, did you ever care for a woman and believe she'd thrown you up? Pass the billy, old man, I'm not up to speaking so much."

He took a long drink at the tea, and then went on.

" 'You love this girl who gave you the ring,' she said. I told her I had cared for her. Then she said 'give it me;' well I couldn't, and I said so.

"She threw it on the ground, and before I could pick it up her heel was on it, and it snapped in two.

"The love of life was indeed broken.

"Then she turned to me—I shan't forget her face—and told me to leave the house. I was going—got to the door—when she fell on the sofa and burst out crying.

"That was kind of rough on me, you know, and I came back again. The first thing I remember was a

pair of hot passionate lips clinging to mine—a soft
low voice whispering in my ear, '*Mon amour! Ma vie!
Je t'aime!*'

"That's how it happened, Harry. I told you she
acted, didn't I? Yes! I married her. It was private,
in the sacristy of the Cathedral. She told me I wasn't
to say I was married just yet, because she had an engagement to play in Sydney, and if they knew it up
there, it would hurt the business.

"See that dog, Harry—guess he sees further with
his shut eyes now, than I did then with mine open.
Devil a word did I say to anyone at all.

"I lived at one end of the town—she at the other.
I saw her home from the church—had dinner. Don't
I mind that dinner! There were green peas—wish we'd
got some for tomorrow. Well, I kissed her—said good
night—and went home.

"That was Monday, October 27, 1873. Tuesday
she went to Sydney—to play an engagement.

"I used to write. It was queer sending letters to
a wife—Harry—and my own at that. I think I used
to write much better ones to other fellow's wives—at
least judging from results.

"One day a telegram came, saying I was to direct
to her in her maiden name, to the Post Office.

It seemed strange. But I thought of her engagement, and did it.

"Did I say she'd a sister? Well, she had. One
day the sister came to me and asked for eight pounds.
Wouldn't tell me what for. I hadn't got it by me;
but I found it soon, and gave it her. Next day I heard
what it was for. My wife had come down suddenly
from Sydney, and wanted the money for expenses.

"Of course I went off directly to see her, but they
said she was too ill, too tired from the sea passage, to
be disturbed from bed. So I took a ring off my hand,
sent it up to her with my love, and left.

"Two days after I did see her. She wrote and asked me to meet her and her mother, and take them out in the gardens.

"I went; but the mother I didn't see. She said she'd follow.

"It was dusk, and the moon was getting up—almost full. I'll remember that night, Harry, as long as I live. We met. She looked pretty, but there was something so cold—so—well, I don't know what about her—that I felt a kind of chill go through me when she spoke. I might have been a friend only.

"The evening set in. It was bright moonlight. We walked on together, not talking much—for married people, who had hardly met.

"We were in the Fitzroy gardens. Fine gardens, too. I could show you the foot of earth we stood on. There were trees all round. It was so quiet, and the moonlight stole through the branches, and threw long shadows over the grass. There was no wind; nothing stirring, nothing near us.

"Harry, did you ever feel it was your duty to love a woman?

"She had never said a kind word to me since we were married; but now she turned in the moonlight and stopped.

"There was a pair of great, big beautiful eyes looking into mine, a pair of little white arms flung around my neck, and in another minute her head fell upon my shoulder, and she burst out crying.

"I'm not stone, Harry. The girl was my wife. I lifted up her head, and kissed her.

"If ever a woman spoke words that a man could construe into love she spoke them then.

"I felt then—she was my wife—it was my duty to love her. I think for the next five minutes I did care about her, and while we stood there, a future I had never thought of opened up—and I was happy.

"She looked so pale, so soft, so womanly, in the moonlight, dressed in light muslin stuff—scarcely looking real—just a little thing like a bunch of flowers for a bonnet, and a thin lace shawl round her, which had fallen upon her waist and hung there.

"Then she kissed me a hundred times—great, long, lingering kisses. Asked me, did I love her?—would I swear to love her always?—never leave her? Could I forgive her faults?—she would be so true to me— would love—did love me with all her heart and soul.

"Harry, did you ever think a woman loved you? It's rough, old man—cursed rough to find out you were wrong.

"Then she talked long and kindly to me; and at last said, with tears in those big, dark eyes, and in her pretty little broken English:

" 'Could you forgive anything in me—anything I had kept from you?'

"She'd an eager, pained look in her face, and she hardly breathed. I thought it was a foolish girl's question. Answered, 'Yes.'

"There was a sound of footsteps on the gravel-path, and the shrill laughter of a little child.

" '*Tiens—Bebe—tiens.*' "

It was her mother's voice!

"For a moment the girl seemed pondering—looking into the future or the past—I knew not which. But suddenly she staggered back, and clasping her hands over her face, cried out—'*Mon Dieu! Mon Dieu!*'

"It was the Past! ! !

"Harry, I'd sooner die a hundred deaths than feel again the pain that shot through my heart just then.

"She fell and fainted on the grass.

"I saw it all. I think there's murder in every man's soul on earth. I knelt over her for a moment. It was in mine then, I knew.

"The horrid, damning, bitter truth, was plain. I thought my head would burst; blood spurted from my mouth and nose. I felt a stifling, suffocating, choking, in my throat; and, with a cry that would come out, I cursed her there and then. I know no more.''

His voice got very low and quiet; and he paused a long painful pause—thinking; then he spoke.

"I think they came and found me there. I turned to look for her, but she was gone.

"The moon was still bright, and beautiful. There was no wind and everything was still. I thought I'd waked up from a dream; but, as I passed my hand across my eyes, I felt there was something on it that wasn't there before.

"It was a thin gold, wedding ring. It's there still, Harry, and she's—ah! God—''

We'd left a shovel behind at the claim that evening. I went to fetch it, and as I crossed the creek, and stumbled through the ferns, a stifled heavy sob came down to me from where the hut lay in the quiet moonlight of that Christmas Eve.

DAGO

Australia again! Well, what does it matter how many years had passed?

Sandy Magee (the coach driver), a bit grayer, a little more furrowed round the eyes, petted and hustled and swore and drove a four-horse team along the deep-rutted bush track between Grafton and Solferino. We were alone; I on the box-seat beside him.

Sandy and I coached that track once before alone together, but we were going the other way then, and I was pretty well broken up, and showed the raw red of healing scars I shall always carry with me. We crossed the old ford on the Clarence again, with the green island a few yards from the bank, and the broad, flat shelf of rock in the middle—with a deep drop into a dozen feet of water a few inches off the near wheels—into which my mate and I went headlong— pack horses and all—the first time we ever attempted it. By the way, we built the first punt that ever carried a dray across it in flood times—a good punt; it floats to-day—and we were driving quietly through old paddocks on the Yugilbar-Ogilve's, the very gum trees of which were familiar. We ring-barked many an acre of those same paddocks, my mate and I, at a price which was never paid us; but that doesn't matter now. Presently we came to a dip, where the track led through heavy timber down a gorge, at the foot of the ranges in which the Solferino diggings lay.

"You remember Dago?" said Sandy, pointing with his whip to a little grass-grown heap of mullock about a dozen yards from the track on our right.

"Do I remember Dago?" Yes, I remembered Dago well. My hand went involuntarily to a heavy scar on my chin. "That's Dago, Sandy," said I pointing to it.

"Well—that's Dago—over there," nodded Sandy with his head. I looked round at the mullock heap, and as I turned, my companion flicked at a blowfly on the off-leader's rump, who, suddenly jumping forward, jerked the old rattle-trap of a coach half across the track.

"Whoa, mare! Whoa! Yes (as we swung into line again at a gallop), that's Dago! Whoa, can't yer?"

But they'd all four got the fidgets, and we flew along the next hundred yards as if the devil was after us.

So that was Dago! It set me thinking—wandering back to New South Wales when I was a lad—a lad on the tramp for gold. Gold I couldn't win in coined sovereigns at home, but with hope in my heart and the dreams of youth, I set out from my ship to dig for from the hard earth of a strange land.

And Sandy told me his memories as we drove through the silent bush. I told Sandy mine in return; and some of the terrible minutes of our lives came back to us both out of the past, and we lived them over again. •

I have had other memorable minutes, but I don't remember so much being crammed into one of them as into that one which flashed back through our minds when Sandy said, "You remember Dago?" Yes, I remembered the city of Grafton, which now revels in a bishop, a cathedral and other appliances of civilization when it was only a straggling bush settlement consisting of one accommodation house, perhaps a dozen weatherboard shanties, a forge and a few tents dotted about at irregular distances from one another on either side of one long, straight, grass-grown street.

But Grafton was looked upon even in those days as quite a "place," for it boasted an annual race meeting and a wharf on the river bank, where once a fortnight a steamer from Sydney used to call, an occurrence of the greatest importance to the entire population, which gathered regularly at the waterside to witness it.

Grafton was the receiving place on the Clarence river for produce coming off the stations to the north; and it suddenly sprang into importance through being the nearest point of debarkation for the new gold rush that broke out at Solferino, a point in the Yugilbar ranges, seventy-five miles away. It was on a scorching day in the seventies that I and my mate, a young Scotchman who had passed for the army, and who, while waiting for his commission, had come out to Australia in the same ship with myself, first set eyes on the place.

We landed, and the same evening left for the diggings by the one long, straggling street, which gradually dwindled away into a track, and soon lost itself in the depths of the primeval bush.

We steered northward by the compass. Besides ourselves there was our dog, a shambling, long-legged, yellow kangaroo hound we called "Jack," and one pack-horse, a raw-boned Waler, christened "Rosinante."

Somehow or other we soon lost the blazed-tree line, the only indication of a way to the gold fields; but after many hardships and mishaps we recovered the track, made Solferino at last, pitched camp, and then settled down to the life of the diggings among some hundreds of others attracted there by the more or less exaggerated reports of the rich "finds" on the reefs.

I still possess my miner's right, which I treasure as a relic of past days. It is reproduced on the following page. There was little or no alluvial gold at Solferino, however, the work being nearly all reefing; and we at once started out to prospect, soon stumbling on a blow-up of gold-bearing quartz, and following it down to a reef which we duly registered as the "Don Juan."

There were six of us in it—my mate, the army officer; Sam Devere, an Irishman and a barrister; Abbott, a smart young fellow who had been in the police; Harry Allen, a Royal Academy of Music man from London, who played divinely on the fiddle and the concertina; "Dago," a Spaniard, and myself.

We picked up "Dago"—as we called him—not because we cared about him, but because we wanted an extra man to make up the six necessary to enable us to apply for a twelve-acre claim along the line of our reef; and "Dago" was loafing around doing nothing. That's how we roped him in. He was rather a sullen chap—dark, handsome, with a black moustache, very white teeth, and a trick of showing them when he smiled, which wasn't often. He talked a little English, of a sort, not unsparsely sprinkled with deities and "big-big-D's," and he camped by himself about a quarter of a mile below the claim on a bend of the Yugilbar creek, where he had put up a log humpy, thatched with sheets of stringy bark.

I strolled down there one Sunday, but he didn't make me welcome, so I never went near him again. "Dago," my mate and I worked in the same shift, two of us down the hole and one on top to wind up.

"Dago" and I had a difference of opinion one night—about a girl, of course. It was Christmas, and they had been having a jamboree in the camp and some dancing. The girl—there were only two altogether on the reefs—gave me a dance, and "Dago" didn't like it. So we quarreled, "Dago" and I, and he gave me some of his special brand of "English." I slipped into him and hurt him. In the middle of my forehead there is a scar—you can see it now—where the haft of the "Dago's" knife caught me in the scrimmage.

There were some words, but our mates separated us, and we went our ways. But "Dago" was never friends after that, and I hated being down the hole with him. Weeks went by, and I had forgotten all about it. I thought "Dago" had, too, but he hadn't, and this is what happened.

We had sunk on the reef about a hundred feet when we came on water, which made so fast that we couldn't work at the bottom of the shaft at all. There was nothing for it but to build a floor about thirty feet up from the bottom and work at that level until the shaft below us was filled up. So we got on.

This floor was simply made of young saplings with the bark left on, laid loosely on a couple of cross-pieces, one at each end of the shaft, which measured the usual six feet by three. The country we were going through was as hard as iron, and we could do nothing with it with the gads and hammers, so started blasting.

It is necessary in order to understand properly what follows for me to describe our work and the way we did it. At the top of the shaft was a windlass, by which one of us hauled up iron buckets from below whilst the other two filled them with stone and mullock as it was broken out. The buckets simply hooked onto an iron hook, which in turn was spliced onto the end of a manila rope working round the windlass-barrel. It was our custom when the bucket was full and hooked on to shake the rope. Then, whoever was at the windlass immediately wound up, and when the bucket reached the top emptied the contents into a paddock and then sent it down below again.

In the shaft we were obliged to blast, as I said before. This was done by drilling holes in the rock, which were then loaded with the blasting powder, the fuse inserted, and then the hole tamped down hard, and fired. The firing was done by lighting a bit of candle over the flame of which we bent the fuse. While the casing of the fuse was burning through whoever fired the shot would have plenty of time to put his foot in the hook, shake the rope and be hoisted up out

of danger. Then off would go the blast, and when the
smoke cleared away we went down again and sent up
the rock broken out by the shot. After we put in the
sapling floor over the water-hole we began to drive
along the face of the reef, and had worked in about a
foot when my gold-mining days were almost brought
to a sudden stop.

My mate, the army man, had injured his hand, and
knocked off work for a spell to get well. So "Dago"
and I had to shift for ourselves. It was my turn down
the hole, and I had succeeded after great labor in put-
ting in two shots about eighteen inches deep, one each
side the shaft where we were driving.

The labor of this was terrific, as, being single-
handed, I had to swing my hammer—an eight-pounder
—with one hand and turn my drill with the other.
However, I got through, loaded up the two holes, bent
my fuses over two pieces of candle, which I lit, and
then shook the rope as the signal to hoist away. Just
as I put my foot in the hook, however, I noticed that
one of the fuses had buckled up with the heat and
turned out of the candle flame, so I stooped down to
bend it straight again. The casing of the other fuse
blazed away merrily, and I knew that in a few seconds
the fuse itself would catch. There was no time to lose.
I turned to grasp the rope—but it was gone!

Looking up the shaft, I saw it disappearing high
above my head. I shouted to "Dago," but he didn't
seem to hear me. The hiss of the fuses, which I had
timed for a half minute, attracted me, fascinated me.
I remember looking helplessly at them, and thinking
I could, perhaps, drag them out. I tried; but no! I
had tamped them in so tight that they would not
budge. My God! What was I to do?

There was about twenty seconds between me and
eternity. I heard nothing but the infernal hissing of
the fuses, and it seemed to get louder and louder.

Suddenly an idea struck me! If I could climb up the shaft I might get above the worst of the blast. I put my back against the face of the shaft and my feet against the other and tried to work up that way. It answered at first. I had got a few feet above the level of the drive when I slipped and came down with a thud on the floor of the shaft.

I heard the saplings crack, but the noise was almost drowned by the awful hissing of the fuses. As I scrambled to my feet a sapling broke under me and my leg went through the floor. With an inspiration, I thought of the well beneath! Still that awful hissing! I knew I had only a few seconds now between me and utter annihilation. I tore away at the saplings like a mad man. My God! how hard they had been jammed down. I saw the water below me; the bright light from the top of the shaft was reflected in it.

Was it my fancy? Did I see "Dago's" face reflected there, or was it my own?

The water was about ten feet down below me. There was no time to hesitate. The only chance of safety lay that way. I made one wild plunge, and as I fell I heard the splitting, hurtling, thundering roar of the blasts as they both went off above me. Then I knew no more.

They told me it was days afterwards when I woke up. I was lying in my humpy, conscious of great pain. My head was all bound up, my left arm was strapped to a piece of wood, and I felt awful.

"Dago's" girl was sitting on a wood heap in the big chimney of the humpy heating something over the fire.

She came up presently beside me and saw I was awake. Dimly the remembrance of something happening in the mine dawned on me.

"What has happened?" I murmured, feebly. She bent down over me. "Hush, you mustn't talk."

"Where's 'Dago'?" I wondered. I must have said it aloud, for she answered——

"Gone!"

"Where?"

"God knows."

The tears welled up in her eyes. Then it all got dark again.

One Christmas Day In Melbourne

Poverty—do I know what poverty means? I set out from England with my heart full of hope and youth for the "Golden South" — Australia — and landed with another "new chum," as the colonists contemptuously call all fresh arrivals from home, thinking to find the place paved with gold and the gutters running with water in which gold dust sparkles.

I had read much about the country—all those fairy tales which are so attractive to the susceptible school-boy, which drive him to the gold fields as surely as Marryat's sea stories drive him to sea.

Well, we landed at Sandridge Pier, cleared from the old ship which had been our home for a completely happy ninety-six days, and started off together to seek our fortunes. My chum had about fifty pounds; I had in all fifteen, but we were young, and these seemed a fortune to us. Melbourne, mavelous Melbourne as it is called, was before us, and we never gave a thought to the morrow.

It was not until our fortunes had dwindled to within an inappreciable distance of zero that we sat one night in solemn conclave over our pipes to discuss the momentous question, What was to be done?

We had to get to work, but what and how? Then came the tug. We presented our letters of introduction and everyone was charmed to see us, asked us to luncheon, to dinner, to supper, to race-meetings, to theatres, everywhere; but the moment we suggested that we were on the lookout for work we became less and less welcome. By degrees we came to have no further use for our dress suits, and they went the way of so many dress suits in the colonies—to our "uncle."

The rest of our store of clothes followed piece by piece, then all our little knicknacks, our shirt studs, our sleeve links, our silk hats, our swagger boots. Why should we burden ourselves with umbrellas and greatcoats? It never rained, and it was hot as hot could be. At length we were left with nothing except what we stood up in, and, on being turned out of lodgings, we parted in the streets of Melbourne.

My mate and I had tossed up to decide which should stop in the city, which take to the bush. He had won the toss and started up country. I was left alone, fourteen thousand miles from home. It was awful to have no friends; as I got shabbier and shabbier my acquaintances dropped me, and I avoided the streets where I might meet them. I felt my poverty was a reproach to myself, and hated to allow anyone to witness it. Gradually I had fallen until I was one of the forlorn band of waifs that every big city possesses—houseless, hungry and hopeless, whose beds at night are in the streets or on the grass under a tree in some public park.

In Melbourne this didn't matter much, for the weather was intensely hot. It was the hunger that was unbearable. Sometimes I earned a few pennies carrying portmanteaux to the station or holding a horse, but frequently for days I earned nothing. I grew miserably thin and hollow-eyed. Try where I would I could get no work.

I was lying one night alongside a man under a tree in the Treasury Gardens. He was as hungry and miserable as I.

"Say, mate, were you ever in jail?" he asked me suddenly.

"No. Why?"

"You can go to jail here for fourteen days, if you like. I've been. It isn't so bad; they feed you well and you only have to crack stones for the roads."

"How can one get there?" I asked.

"I've got a chum at the police station. He'll put us down as vagrants. You don't have to steal anything.

I was horribly hungry. "All right, come on," I said.

It was Christmas Eve. We stood by the gates of the Gardens in the moonlight. We heard the town clock in the distance striking midnight, and as the last stroke died away the bells of St. Patrick's Cathedral pealed out, and down the deserted street came the chant through the open doors proclaiming God's promise of "Peace on earth, good will to men."

I thought of my own dear England, of home, of my dear father and sisters so many miles away, and the tears welled up in my eyes.

"My God, I can't stand this!" said my mate, and he fled down the street into the quiet of the night.

The river shone like a silver streak in the moonlight, and I knew what he meant. I walked to the great steps of the Cathedral, and through the doors I saw the lights of the great high altar and the priests chanting the mass. Everything seemed to be swimming around me. I remember the voices, the heavy perfume of the incense. I heard the "Gloria in Excelsis Deos," and then I remember no more.

When I came to I found myself in a small room with an old priest kneeling by my side. God bless him, wherever he is? He is one I shall never forget, for he started me fair on my road in life. From that day to this when I feel dismayed and weak the tender voice and kindly smile of this dear old man come back to me, and with them the memory of that Christmas Day in Melbourne when St. Patrick's bells rang out the welcome "Peace on earth, good will to men!"

MINE HAUS

Up in the diggings, and in fact pretty well all over the colonies, the good, old, genteel Elizabethan oath, "By our Lady!" has been contracted by frequent usage to "Bloody!" and formed three parts of the common language. Apparently there was no adjective or number of them considered so comprehensive. No sentence was complete without it. It was applied to everything—long, short, tall, thick or thin, high or low, deep or shallow, far or near, white, black or any color, quick or slow, good, bad or indifferent. There was no place where it was not dragged into service, except perhaps in the churches or public schools. And as there was no church at Maytown and the school-house was way off on a hill by itself, the refining influences of these two exceptional establishments were without effect.

If a penny had really been put in the tin can with a slit in the lid every time that particular oath was used in the bar of "Mine Haus" its landlord could long ago have retired from business. But his invitation to his patrons to fine themselves this modest sum each time they swore had gone disregarded for years, and the tin can stood upon the bar counter as a curio rather than as a regulator of the language and morals of Maytown. Though the landlord who had first placed it there still ran the "pub," the miners swore unpunished, because for years it was "the only bloody pub in a hundred bloody miles."

"Mine Haus," as he called it, had been kept for years—in fact ever since the "good times" at Maytown—by a thick-set little German named Ahlers. He had several sons and daughters—one in the "sem-

terry," so he said; one in a convent at Cooktown learning "bianner und bainting"; one son was a miner on
his own account, and another carried the mail round
to Palmerville, a route of over two hundred miles, and
he did it every week. So they all worked hard.

Ahlers also had a wife who went by the name of
"Mine Vife," and dog he called "Shmoker."

The Prince of Wales Hotel, the official name of
"Mine Haus"—stood in the middle of the right-hand
side of the only street in Maytown. On its left was a
dilapidated and empty shanty that in the "good
times" used to be the Queensland National Bank, and
on its right was a vacant lot covered with empty meat
and jam tins. Among these a few dirty aboriginees
squatted, smoking stumpy old bits of broken pipes—
and the goats browsed. Beyond this was the hut of a
Chinaman—he was the cook at "Mine Haus"—and
beyond that two tumbledown shanties, which ended the
street.

The other side was occupied by three Chinese stores
and by a place that in the old days was a "pub," but
which at the time of this incident was inhabited by a
man and his wife who acted as caretakers of a lot of
worn-out old mining machinery; also of the premises
of the deserted bank before mentioned. This family
was notable chiefly for a lot of squalling children and
for one fat daughter who played upon a broken-down
piano with one finger. Below them was chaos and
goats as far as Paddy Fahy's, which had lately blos-
somed into a licensed house where drinks cost only
sixpence as against a shilling at "Mine Haus."

Because of this there was war between "Mine
Haus" and "Dot Damned Irish Shanty," where drinks
cost but sixpence, for it is cheaper to get drunk at
sixpence a drink than at double that, a fact that Maytown did not take long to grasp. The landlord of
"Mine Haus" could recollect the time when the mid-

day meal tables "vas full mit von hundert und vorty to vifty miners—efery day! Und dere vas vifteen pubs vot I could count from mine door—zo it vas— und dey vas drink all night, ain't it? Und now I vas tell you, for Gosstruth, I cannot make de zwei ends meet—und dot damned Irish shanty below sellin' der visky und grog for sixpence, ain't it?

"Noaw Harry, vot you vas krumble for zo moch? You ought ter pe 'shamed mit yerself komparing dot low-down shanty mit de Printz obt Vales, so you ought. Get out, Shmoker! Vot I told you? Haf I not toldt it you to get out mit you?" And poor "Shmoker, warned by the dulcet-toned voice of "Mine Vife," would just escape the broom handle and Harry's foot as he scuttled out of the dining room, over the veranda and into the street.

"Dere gets avay dot damnt dog akain! Shmoker, kom here! Kom here! Do you hear me? I vas shain you op mit youself!" And poor "Shmoker" would slink back, to be chained up beneath the water tank in a corner of the yard, where he could see no one and amuse himself with nothing except a stray duckling, which persistently waddled over to the wet ground beneath the leaky tap to fancy itself in a pond.

Poor old Shmoker! He was a sad mongrel, with a long nose that turned up and a tail about an inch out of the proper line—of no breed at all except that in some forgotten age an ancestor must have casually met with an Irish terrier. But Shmoker and I were pals. I used to take him bits of bread, talk doggie-talk to him, and scratch his back with a stick just where the ticks were and he couldn't reach. He loved that.

Shmoker wouldn't let a nigger or a Chinaman near the place at night without raising Cain, so that was where he came in and what made him "vorth his tucker" to "Mine Haus." But he led an awful life;

so did the ducks and the geese and the fowls, although
you wouldn't think it to see them all cluster about
Ahlers when he came down the yard each day with a
can of corn. For one old duck had a broken wing,
and the hens and geese knew more about broom handles
than did even poor Shmoker, and one and all they
knew "Gott in Himmel" and "Gott tam" as well as
they knew the broom.

Such was the sad state of affairs at "Mine Haus"
when the miners began to desert it. But there was one
crowd living out at the "Comet," headed by Bob
Jenkins and his brother Jack, that rode in to it regularly every week for a good drink. They did not
patronize "Paddy Fahy's," because their account at
Ahler's had grown so big they hadn't the face. They
had not the money to "wipe the slate."

Besides Bob and Jack Jenkins there was Isaac
Brown, who looked upon himself as "King of Maytown," because he was "our own correspondent" for
the Cooktown Independent. Brown used to call an
accident "a melancholy catastrophe," and he announced the arrival of Mrs. Brown's baby as "a son
and heir was ushered into the world." Oh, Brown
was a great man! He had a long, black, bushy beard,
of which he always chewed the ends, and a "breath"
that he had been cultivating "on the cheap" for many
years, in fact ever since he had lost his first wife.

To go back to Bob Jenkins: Bob ran a battery out
at the "Comet." It belonged to another man—nobody
knew how he got it—but now and then he would cart
headings to it from some old claim and have a crushing. All Maytown knew when Bob had a good crushing, and Ahlers was delighted, for he had visions of
Bob's score being wiped out—but it never was. Bob
got drunk all the same, however.

Bob had just finished a crushing that cleaned up
badly. He had put through about fifty tons, but there

was the firewood and the carting to be counted. As he put it, "The God damned stuff only went five bloody weights and all my bloody work gone for a whole bloody fortnight."

Well, after this crushing, Bob and Jack rode into Maytown together, rounded up Isaac, "shouted" for old Ahlers and Charley, who had just come in "off the census," and lounged all together into the bar of "Mine Haus," where they got down to business.

"Vy you fellers no go down mit the Irish shanty, ain't it?" asked Ahlers after the third round.

"Oh, damn the Irish shanty," answered Bob. "Look here, Ahlers, you and me's known each other for years and I've allers drunk at this bloody pub, and I ain't a-goin' to shift down to that bloody shanty anyway."

"Vell, Bob, I alvays haf done my best for you. You can't say that I haf not, can yer?"

"No bloody fear, Harry, I can't. Come on, let's have another. Wot's it to be? Here, Charley, wot's yours? Jack, fill up again. Isaac?"

Isaac broke in sharply, "Same!" He never let a chance slip.

"You, Harry, wot are yer goin' to do?"

"Shoost the same, Bob, shoost the same."

And so it went until Charley Ahlers said he was going home.

"G'long!" It was about ten o'clock now and Bob and Jack were both drunk.

"G'long!" said Bob. "Have another."

"No, Bob, no more."

"You're no bloody good, you ain't," cried Jack.

"I'm as good as you and chance it." Charley laughed.

"I'm damned if you are."

"Yes, I am, and you know it."

"Put yer bloody hands up and see," shouted Jack, "you—you—"

"Mein Gott, Bob, no fightin' here!"

"Oh, you go to hell, you bloody Dutchman."

"Look here, Jack, don't you go to insulting my father!" chirped up Charley, getting a bit ugly.

"I say he kin go ter Hell and you with him. Come out in the road and I'll belt Hell out of yer and every bloody Dutchman in the place."

"Yer can do it, too, Jack, can't yer?" yelled Bob, now gloriously drunk.

"My bloody colonial oath!"

"Well, you keep a civil tongue in yer head, Jack—that's all," and Charley turned away to go.

"Ah, yer bloody Dutch whelp—take that!" and Jack lunged viciousy at young Ahlers, hitting him heavily.

Now, Charley was one of those long-limbed, wiry, sinewy Colonials, used to working hard, seldom drinking and leading a decent sort of a life. Once roused, however, he was a terror, and now he was fairly roused.

The fight didn't last long, for Jack fell about all over the place while Charley pounded him.

O'Reagan, the constable, strolled down when he thought that the fight had gone as far as did good, and separated the men. He summoned Bob and Jack to appear in court the next day for creating a disturbance and using obscene language in a public place, and it cost Bob and Jack about three pounds in fines and costs.

But Bob found another thing yet a bitterer pill to swallow. Father Ahlers, having been summoned as a witness, appeared against him. When it was all over Bob made straight for the old German and shook his fist in his face.

"Never again—so help me—will I touch another bloody drop in your bloody house," he yelled. "By God, and this is what you call gratitude! And I—I—*I've kept your bloody house open for years!*"

"Und how?" cried the furious old man, "und how? *Mit a slate!*"

Next week Bob took his cargo aboard at "dot damned Irish shanty," but when too drunk to move or be moved he coiled himself up on the verandah of "Mine Haus." Here Paddy Fahy saw him and chuckled.

How I Got On the Stage

Good Lord, how it rained! It wasn't a shower or a squall; it came down in bucketsful; the whole reservoir of Heaven seemed to have burst and emptied the accumulated water of centuries upon our devoted decks. I was one of the mates of a big passenger liner, a large three-masted, ship-rigged vessel with double top-gallant yards, not then so much in use as they are today. She was the "Thomas Stevens," one of the quickest and smartest ships afloat with passengers from Melbourne to London. We were swinging into position to enter the Milwall docks. My foot touched land for the first time for ninety days when I leaped from the rail onto the dolphin at the Dock gates, slipped the end of our guess-warp over the bollard, and sang out to them inboard to take in the slack.

"Hullo!" came a hail from the pier-head, muffled by the mist and noise of the falling rain.

I looked around. On the pier I could see indistinctly a few miserably wet-looking men and one or two dockhands comfortably enveloped in oilskins, off which the water poured in torrents.

"Hullo!" came the hail again. "Hullo, is that you, Harold?"

Harold was my name right enough, but I didn't know who on earth could be hailing me. I had been out in Australia for nearly five years. My dear father was dead. My sisters were married; one was in India, the other with her husband's regiment God knows where, and my elder brother had been in Canada for many years, and for all I knew was still there. I hadn't a friend in the world I could expect to greet me. Though I heard my name, I thought there must be some man among the passengers with the same name, so I took no notice. When the ship swung alongside the dolphin

I jumped aboard into the mizzen-rigging and then, just as I reached the deck, out of the mist came the hail again.

"Hullo, Harold, is that you?"

I turned and peered through the rain. A slight, clean-shaven man stood on the pier-head waving a stick. God, how wet he was! I looked again. There was something familiar about him. The voice, too, I seemed to have heard before.

The ship was creeping nearer every moment, and the figures ashore getting more distinct. Out of the mist came the voice again:

"Is Harold Bellew on board?"

There was no mistake about that anyway. I turned and sang out, "Yes, who are you?"

"Evelyn," came the answer.

It was my brother. We had not met for thirteen years. We stood staring at each other speechless.

When we got alongside he climbed aboard. He had heard by some means that I had shipped on the "Thomas Stephens" and come down to meet me at the dock. I was enveloped in oilskins, and he, poor chap, was soaked to the bone. We couldn't speak, either of us, and I felt a lump in my throat, and was glad it was raining. Hurrying him into my berth to put on some of my dry clothes, I returned on deck to my duties, which would end when the decks were cleared up.

"That will do, men," sang out the mate.

Wet as they were, the hands tumbled over the side and went off in a body to get their first drink at a little public house outside the gates.

"What are you going to do, Mr. Bellew?" asked the mate as we walked aft together.

"I don't know till I get ashore."

I had shipped only for the run home, and I knew the owners would have another man of their own to take my place on the ship's next voyage.

My brother and I were about the same size, so my clothes fitted him all right. "Where shall I go?" I asked him.

"I have a room up in Maida Vale, near dad's old church. Come there with me, old chap."

So I went.

We had sorry stories to tell each other. He was down to his last penny, and I, after the ship paid off, found myself the possessor of just eight pounds in the world. We divided the money and then discussed the past. Poor old fellow! he's dead now. He had made just as big a mess of life as I had, worse even, for he had greater chances which he had thrown to the winds. He had gone to America with McHenry, the great railroad magnate, and might have done anything, for he was a splendid engineer. But he had got bitten by an absurd stage fever and thrown up everything to follow the fortunes of a company of players in Toronto. How many years he had been roaming about doing what he could to keep body and soul together he didn't say. But, at my father's death, he had come home, and when we met on that pelting wet August morning he was literally strapped.

We discussed the question what was to be done.

"I can't get anything to do. The theatrical managers won't look at me," he told me. The truth was, poor chap, he never was a good actor.

"I must go back to engineering," he admitted, "but how—how—how? Every billet seems to be full."

He scanned the columns of the Daily Telegraph. There were lots of "Wanteds." He told me he had answered hundreds until he was sick of being turned down and of getting no answers to his letters.

In the middle of one column my eyes fell upon the following advertisement, which I read out aloud:

STAGE—Wanted, a light comedian
to support Miss Helen Barry on tour,
commencing August 22d. Apply per-
sonally to Charles Barrington, Esq.,
Adelphi Hotel, Adams Street, Strand.

"Won't that do?" I asked him.

"Good God, that's been there for a week. I've sat
on the doorsteps of the Adelphi for hours only to get
turned down for my pains."

"Well," said I, "I haven't got a ship. I don't see
any chance of getting one. I won't go before the mast.
I can't starve, and I haven't any money except these
few sovereigns. I'm the lightest comedian I know just
now and I'm going to have a shot at Charles Barrington, Esquire."

My brother laughed at me. "What sort of a chance
have you got?" he cried.

"There are lots of damned fools who know no
more than I do and get billets every day in other busi-
nesses. I'll have a try, anyway."

"If you give your name as 'Bellew' he'll turn you
down at once. He will think it is I and refuse to see
you."

"That's easily fixed. I'll send in my Christian
name, 'Harold Kyrle.' That sounds like a theatrical
name, anyway."

After considering the matter further it was agreed
that I should go to the Adelphia the next morning and
try my luck. I had no clothes except what I had been
wearing at sea. My best coat, a blue serge, bore the
gilt anchor-buttons the company insisted that its officers should wear. We went out, and finding a little
tailor's shop where "Repairs Neatly Executed" was
posted in the window, we went in, and the little tailor
soon clipped off my buttons and in their place sewed a
set of neat plain black ones. Barring my cap, which

bore the company's badge, I was now turned into a civilian.

"Now for a pot-hat," cried I, "and I'm all ready to pass for a 'light comedian.'"

The eventful morning arrived. At half-past ten I found myself ushered into the presence of a very pale, thin-faced, clean-shaven, mouse-colored man who was sitting at a table busy opening letters taken from a pile scattered in front of him. He looked up for an instant, and then, resuming his work, said in rather a soft, pleasant voice:

"You wish to see me, Mr.—Mr.—?"

"Kyrle, Harold Kyrle, sir," I broke in as he took up the little piece of paper on which my name was written.

"Kyrle—Kyrle, I don't think I know the name," he said, still gazing at the piece of paper. "What can I do for you?" He settled back, his elbows resting upon the arms of his chair and joining the tips of his fingers, looked me up and down.

I was bronzed, hard as a nail and salt-pickled—a direct contrast to the anaemic gentleman before me. I remember feeling a kind of pity for him, he looked so weak and puny.

"I came to see Mr. Charles Barrington in answer to this advertisement in the Daily Telegraph.

"Oh!" said he, "I am Mr. Barrington. Are you a light comedian? I don't remember your name."

"Probably not," I answered; "I only arrived from Australia a couple of days ago."

"Australia? Oh! Have you had much experience out there?"

Experience! thought I to myself. I had been in every mortal thing a man could be except in gaol. As he failed to specify what kind of experience, I answered boldly:

"Any amount."

"Ah! They change the bill very frequently out
there—stock companies, I believe?"

"Very frequently," I replied, which was quite true.

"It must be very hard work, I should imagine."

I assented.

Our conversation continued in this way for some
time. During it all he never asked me once directly
or indirectly whether I had ever been upon the stage,
so I felt my conscience perfectly clear in conforming
my answers to the questions he put without volunteer-
ing anything else.

At last Mr. Barrington seemed satisfied. "Well,
Mr. Harold Kyrle," he said, "I think you will suit me.
Go round to Blackmore's, the agents, in Garrick Street,
give him this note and he will give you a contract.
The salary will be two pounds per week. We find cos-
tumes, except wigs, shoes, stockings, swords, jewelry
and laces. Will that suit you?"

Anything would have suited me! With a profusion
of thanks in my heart, which I carefully concealed
from him, I bowed myself out of Mr. Charles Barrington's presence and walked out into the strand.

My poor brother was waiting for me nearby. When
I told him of my success he stared at me open-mouthed.

"Well, I'm damned!" he said.

"All right, old chap, don't anticipate things," I
responded gleefully. "Now let's go up to this bally
agent's, or whatever he is, 'sign on,' and then we'll
go and 'wet' the commission. Where is Blackmore's?"

"You don't mean to say that he has made you go
to Blackmore's?" exclaimed my brother.

"He has. Why shouldn't he?"

"Only that Blackmore will take ten per cent of
your miserable salary for ten weeks, that is all."

"The devil he will," cried I.

"It's a sort of authorized custom of the profession,"
explained my brother. "You'll have to submit until

you are strong enough to tell the agents all to go to the Devil.''

I determined that time should come—and it did eventually.

To make a long story short, I went to the agent's and came away with a contract in my pocket to play light comedy on a provincial tour under the management of Mr. Charles Barrington for two pounds a week. And I was mulcted of ten shillings and ten per cent. of my salary for ten weeks, just for the privilege of inscribing my name on Mr. Blackmore's books.

But anyway, I was a full-fledged actor now! Ten days later I found myself, about half-past eight at night, walking onto the stage of the Theatre Royal, Brighton, dressed up in a gorgeous costume of pale blue and silver, and with a long fair-haired wig upon my head, acting ''Lord Woodstock'' in Tom Taylor's successful and picturesque play, ''Clancarty.''

The papers the next morning—shall I ever forget them?—said I ''played splendidly.''

The moral of this story is doubtful, but it only goes to show what a sailor with a face like a brazen image and illimitable cheek can do when put to it.

HEN AND CHICKEN

They were very hard up, for times were bad in the theatre world, and nobody seemed to want either one or the other. But no one knew it except themselves. They used to look helplessly into each other's eyes every morning, when he would come up from his dingy little home to where she lived, to see if, Micawber-like, anything had turned up.

"Nothing, Chicken?"—his name for her.

"Nothing, Hen!"—her name for him.

And another hopeless day would drag along.

So it went for months.

They had been pals for years—players together all over the world—won together—rejoiced together—suffered together—and he had watched over her just like an old hen over her one chicken.

So she called him "Hen-mother," then "Hen" for short.

And now things looked very blue.

In early life he had been at sea, but drifted away into the Australian bush, while his ship lay at Sandridge Pier and a new rush broke out. The rush was way up north on the Palmer; plenty of gold and lots of fever; he got some of both, and it became a question whether to get rich and die or get out. So he "humped his drum" to the coast. *But he had seen gold.* One day, camping at noon, he knocked a piece of stone off the cap of a reef which showed colors freely.

Gold had come too late! He crawled away along the ghastly track through Maytown to Hell's Gates and on to Cooktown where he stowed away on a ship bound south.

They played together in Australia years afterwards, and he often spent an hour telling her of the old life on the Palmer River. They did well, made money and came back to London, where things prospered for them both, until one awful November day when she said she "felt gray"—and for three months doctors watched her hanging between life and death. Every night on his way to the theatre he would look up into the murky London sky and pray God for her life. And God was very good and listened, and he thanked God from his heart. It was soon after this that things got so bad, and they came across a man they had known in the Colonies and all got to talking gold.

"I know where there's gold," said Hen.

"Where?"

"Up on the Palmer."

"Palmer's abandoned years ago."

"So was Bendigo once."

"How do you know gold's up there?"

"I've seen it."

"But it's all worked out."

"I don't think so."

And they looked over Dr. Jack's latest geological map and found no reef marked where Hen said there was gold.

"There's a fortune up there." Hen put his finger on a spot that lay about twenty-six miles to the south-east of Maytown.

"Why don't you go and get it if you're so sure?"

And the man laughed.

And the "Chicken" sighed.

And the "Hen" folded up the map and put it way.

But a few weeks later, at the "Stores," he and she were buying a few cheap necessaries for some one who was going into the tropics.

"I want a pillow of some sort—anything will do," said Hen.

There were many sorts to choose from, but all seemed very dear, they thought, for money was very scarce. That friend whom they had told had lent Hen enough to get out to the Palmer.

"I want you to have a comfortable pillow, Hen. What does it matter—a few shillings—and it will be so much better. Flock gets into such horrid lumps—and it's so hot and stuffy—horse-hair will keep you cool."

"How much are these horse-hair pillows?" asked Hen.

"A guinea, sir."

Hen looked up and drew a quick breath.

Chicken sighed.

"That settles it! Flock—three and six—will do for me."

Chicken turned away and seemed very interested in an advertisement of somebody's soap. When she thought no one noticed, she quickly brushed her cheek with her handkerchief. *She* had a horse-hair pillow at home.

But Hen-mother had seen. When they left the "Stores," he chaffed about feather pillows and such luxuries, and told her that a clean sheet of Stringy-bark with a saddle for a pillow made as comfortable a bed as anyone could possibly want in the bush.

He was going back again—after twenty years—to look for gold. It seemed a wild idea, a hopeless sort of scheme, this going out to Australia, but they had talked it over and thrashed it out and is seemed best. And so one day he came up in the morning for the last time. It was ten o'clock, and his ship was to sail from the Albert Dock at twelve.

For the first time in twelve years they were parted.

On the ship he commenced a diary and the opening words were: January 18, 1900. The most miserable day of my life.

Weeks after, when he got her first letter, which was written the day he left, he read through dim eyes.

"My Hen-mother—I couldn't see anyone—I just locked my door—and threw myself down on my bed—and buried my face in the pillow—and then I thought of your poor old head on the horrid flock pillow—and my heart broke.   .   ."

He had an old photograph of her he always carried, and, sitting in his tent at the Laura River thousands of miles away, he looked at it and kissed the beautiful face it pictured to him.

Time went on. Fortune seemed turning for them both. She had one or two good offers in London and wrote out, "Don't worry, my Hen, about me. If the piece is a success I shall be all right." And it was a success.

And he wrote home to her, "I am in luck. I found the old spot where I camped years ago and broke the stone. The country is wild, unutterably wild and lonely. There is nothing within miles of me. I am absolutely alone. I have worked on the reef, which is a very fine one, and shows gold freely. It is on the top of a spur, and the other day I was fossicking in the gully below when I came across some nice little pieces of gold. But it is lonely—lonely—lonely—beyond words."

Months went by until one day she received a cable from Reuter and her heart stood still. She trembled and hesitated to open it for it was from Australia. What had happened?

She shut herself up and turned the key in the door, then knelt down by the desk where she kept all her letters and murmured, "God grant there is nothing wrong!" Then she opened the envelope and read the cable.

"Maytown.

Have cabled you one thousand pounds today. Paris
Bank. Well. HEN.''
Then she cried.

She didn't know what to do she felt so happy.
She had been a bit ill, but all that seemed to vanish
and everyone at the theatre that night thought she was
''Splendid!''

The gully turned out to be a regular bonanza, and
for weeks he worked on alone until he had stripped it
from end to end. The creek near where he camped ran
all the year, and from morning till dark he panned and
worked the ''pay dirt,'' until there was no more to
pan.

At first he used to hide the gold in his flock pillow,
which had got into hard lumps itself, hardly distin-
guishable from the nuggets. And as the pile grew and
there were no more soft spots for his head, he used to
laugh and think, ''I wonder if Chicken would rather
I kept my pillow now than change it for a horse-hair
one?

He didn't know how much gold there was. When
the pillow got too full, he dug a hole under his camp
and buried it all. Then he went in to Maytown and
told the Warden he had found gold on the creek.

There was a rush and the papers heard of it. ''Revival of the Palmer,'' announced one. ''Big Find Near
Maytown,'' another.

Hen pegged out a fifty-acre lease of the reef he had
found twenty years before and called it the ''Hen and
Chicken.'' Then in a little time he got some gunny
bags, filled them with stone from the reef and in each
he put another bag full of the gold he had won from
the gully and buried in his tent. Chinamen ''packed''
these bags down to the Laura River for him; from
there they were never out of his reach to Cooktown,
where he sailed on the same ship with them for Brisbane. Here he opened the big bags and took out the

little bags of gold before sending the quartz to Aldershot to be crushed and assayed.

A couple of weeks later the sensation of the evening paper in Brisbane was as follows:

> Two tons of stone from the "Hen and Chicken" reef near Cannibal Creek, on the Palmer Gold Field, were crushed at Aldershot for the phenomenal return of 757 ounces of retorted gold. This reef was taken up by a gentleman from London who, in the early days of the Palmer discovered it while tramping on his way to Cooktown, to which place he was proceeding, almost dying from fever. This was twenty years ago, and the gentleman in question had the good luck recently to rediscover the reef which is in the wildest part of the ranges to the S. E. of Maytown, and which had eluded the notice of prospectors from that day until its recent discovery. Provision has been made to float the "Hen and Chicken" into a company in London, a very high price having been offered for it on the advice of a well-known London expert, who was fortunate enough to be in Cooktown lately on his way to examine some New Guinea property."

Hen traveled by the first P. & Q. boat that started after he had lodged the gold in the bank and received a draft for it on London payable at ninety days to Chicken. His Palmer gold proved to be as good as any in the world and fetched over four pounds an ounce at the Sydney Mint.

So now, what with the gold itself and the purchase money for the mine, he was rich. As he came over the gangway of the steamer, a rather disreputable-looking digger's "swag" was being hoisted on board. Lashed to this were a pick, a shovel and a pan, with labels on them, "Sydney to London." They were old friends that had "seen him through," and in the heart of the "swag" was a very much worn and clay-stained flock pillow.

"I'll keep the old traps as curios," he said to the third officer, who asked him why on earth he was shipping such a kit as that.

It was midsummer when he reached home and she was living up the river where he found her one glorious evening looking radiantly beautiful and happy. They would neither of them speak—their hearts were too full—and the tears started to their eyes as their hands met. At last he said:

"Chicken, I have brought home something for you —here it is." And he put his hand in his pocket and from an old worn leather case produced a faded photograph of her, round which was wrapped a draft for twelve thousand pounds.

"It helped to stuff my pillow along with the flock."

They both laughed nervously.

He held out the paper. Mechanically she took it and saw what it was, then wanted to speak but no words came. She was choking but, dimly, through the rush of her own feelings saw the tears trickle down his gaunt, bronzed cheeks. Then all got blurred and she sobbed out, her heart clasped close in his arms.

They were drifting in a punt alone on the river. In the moonlight, he had told her all his life since he had left her a year ago and she had told him all hers. He was still a young man as men go, and she in the prime of her beauty and womanhood. He had loved her for years but he had been too poor to talk of anything to her but work.

"What will you get from the "Hen and Chicken?"" she asked.

They sat together on the cushions in the middle of the punt. He turned the paddle slightly with which he steered. "All told about a hundred and thirty to a hundred and fifty thousand." He turned, looked into her beautiful eyes in the moonlight and smiled happily. "Half of that's yours, Chicken."

"Mine!"

"Yes—we're 'mates'—we've always been 'mates' and out in Australia your 'mate' always has half of everything."

"Oh, that's absurb, Hen. Half a loaf when you haven't anything else—or half—half—" She couldn't think of anything else just then.

"We were 'mates,' dear, when I went away and if we aren't to remain 'mates,' I wish I had never gone. It has been awful—alone in the bush—never seeing you. I have been away a whole year and you have had to fight it out alone when I might have been here to help you."

"But you have helped me—more than you could have done by staying by me."

"Then I am content, at least—"

"At least?"

"Almost."

"What more can you want?"

"Can't you guess, Chicken?" His voice was very tender, very low and carried her thoughts back for years to the night when first she played "Juliet" to his "Romeo," and he murmured to her in the Balcony Scene in a voice that woke an echo in her own heart which had sounded there ever since. But to her he had always been "Hen-mother." She was like a child; she had told him all her troubles, all her joys; to him her word, her wish was a law, and yet they were 'mates' who had grown necessary to each other, although they had never spoken of love.

"I know—" she said it very tenderly, as she took his hand and nestled a little closer. "I know—you want me to give you a horse-hair pillow in place of your old flock one."

He looked round. Her eyes were infinitely gentle,

her head had sunk down on his shoulder and her face was turned up to his in the moonlight.

"Yes—beloved—" He spoke very slowly and drew her closer to him. He could just hear her whisper:

"You shall have mine !"

How We Pegged Buchanan

Hughes had beautiful sentiments and a faraway look in his eyes. Sometimes he washed and shaved; at such times, he was quite good looking. Then again, sometimes he didn't, this generally after a drunk. His drunks occurred on Sundays, Mondays, Tuesdays, Wednesdays, Thursdays, Fridays and Saturdays, with one occasion every four years—the 29th of February, his birthday—on which he did himself proud. Hughes had a standard joke that he was only eight, because he had lived the round of only eight leap-years. He was really thirty-three and regretted that he hadn't had thirty-three real birthdays to celebrate.

When he told you all his beautiful thoughts about honest dealing with his fellowmen and such like, you felt a certain qualm over the fifty acre lease you pegged out the day before he intended to take it up himself, but then, "you were the only man he cared to see hold ground near his, and anyway it wasn't of any value as the reef didn't dip that way, so it didn't matter."

When Hughes clapped you on the shoulder, "old man," and told you this your conscience left off bothering, but you knew you had better keep your weather eye on Hughes. He never wore socks, but he was very kind to Isaac Brown's kids, and he had a pet possum which nestled inside his shirt and seemed fond of him. Possums are very hardy.

I believe Hughes was married, but he never had any wife on the diggings. His clothes were worse than most of us wore, and he generally went round without a hat. The sun never seemed to affect him, though "next morning" he always said it had.

His strong point, he thought, was geology, so the boys brought his wonderful bits of rock which he duly sent down South for assay, receiving in return very rude letters about them which puzzled him. But Hughes did stumble across something once, though by accident. An old German prospector died and left behind a small lease which he had been working. The water had been bad in the well he sank, and the old fellow had grown worse and worse, dying eventually of arsenical poisoning.

Now arsenical poisoning meant very little to Hughes, but a great deal to Cameron and Pegus, who were always sniffing around for anything "good," and quickly scented arsenical pyrites. So Cameron, Pegus, Hughes and a borrowed Chinaman soon had the old German's lease looking as though a lot of Gullivers had been playing cribbage on it and using gigantic matches for pegs. And they wern't satisfied.

Higgins was a quiet old chap who knew a good bit about mining. He had been out to Buchanan several times nosing round. He pegged out 75 acres at Mount Madden—more as a blind, I think, than anything else —and one day drove his pegs home on Buchanan, when no one was about. But Hughes and his gang disputed him and Pegus, one of them, being Warden of the Field, had laid official hands upon it.

Higgins was a hard-faced old man, who looked at life between the lies and the jokes as rather a serious thing. He lived at Ahlers' but never drank anything, so he was referred to when out of earshot disrespectfully as "Dot damned old Higgins." He came in to meals regularly and never passed anything. When Ahlers wanted to be satirical he would refer to the climate as being "Splendid for yong beebles und old men," and with a look at Higgins that it "gaf. von healthy abetites."

"I'll trouble you for a bit more of that steak, Jimmy," was all the answer old Higgins gave, and Jimmy, the Chinese cook, would laugh serenely and bring the steak.

I sat next to Higgins. The old music box on the table between the windows just behind me had a way of going off unexpectedly with three bars of "Annie Laurie" and then petering out. Every man within a hundred miles had shaken bits of "Annie Laurie" out of that old box, which was one of the stories of Maytown, together with the worsted-worked pictures of Koenig Wilhelm and a stuffed crocodile out of the Mitchell River. The piano in the corner was a compound fractured instrument, of German origin, that emitted nothing but Wagnerian noises whether you played "God Save the Queen" or "Hail, Columbia!" on it. Ahlers had lent it to Isaac Brown for a dance some ten years before. It had been dropped on the way down hill, and the sounding board broken in two. Bob Jenkins, blacksmith from the "Comet," had come to its rescue and a sailorman "who knew how to splice wire," had fixed the other part. Then a traveling dentist who did something to Mrs. Ahlers' teeth had a go at it.

This made it ready for Miss Ahlers to play. Miss Ahlers was a big girl with a "musical ear." Where the music box left off with "Annie Laurie" she went on and thumped out the rest on "Old Wagner." She helped the "black gin" make the beds when she wasn't busy playing "Annie Laurie," but that wasn't often. My first recollection of Maytown, is rolling out of my saddle to "Annie Laurie" and, as I rode down hill on my way "home" among the "so longs!" "come back some days!" and "don't forget us alls," I caught the strain of "Annie Laurie" with every other tooth out.

But to go back to Higgins: He had confided with me that he believed that Hughes and his gang had pegged out the wrong ground at Buchanan, and that the lode lay more to the eastward. So I had promised to go out with him and take up the more promising ground on the following Monday.

This was Saturday, and everyone was in camp for an incidential drunk and to wait over Sunday for the arrival of the mail. The day was fading when Hughes sat down beside me on Ahlers' verandah, and began poking out quartz pebbles with the butt end of a piece of iron-bark.

"Damned hot!" said Hughes.

"Not so damned," I grunted for the sake of argument.

Long pause while he pushed out another pebble. Then he threw one at the dog. "Shmoker" knew he was quite safe, so he lay still.

"Been out at the Queen to-day?" Hughes looked far away where the sun was setting behind the hills and drew squares in the soft red earth.

"No."

Another long pause, then, "I just came in from Buchanan," he said.

"So!" I knew it already, but I saw Hughes was leading for an opening.

"Fine show out there—why don't you go and have a look at it?"

"Heard you'd got it all." Hughes looked at me. I felt it.

"There's lots more to the eastward. Hughes drew another square.

"Why don't you take it up them?"

"Oh, I don't know. . . . Got a match?"

"I should if I thought it good. . . . Yes, here's one."

"Heard you were going out Monday with Higgins."

"Did you?"

"Yes." Hughes lit his pipe. The light in the west was failing fast.

"Well, perhaps I will."

"Going to peg out?" As the match flared up between the puffs, I could see Hughes' little beady eyes squinting out of their corners at me.

"I might."

Then there was another long pause. It was almost dark and the lights of the camp here and there stood out like gems against the deep of the moonless sky. Shmoker saw the Chink's cat—otherwise all was hushed and still.

Hughes finally broke the silence. "I thought of taking up that ground to the east," he announced, "but I wired to Melbourne and they said, 'No.' It ain't any good anyhow, shouldn't advise you to peg there. I tried a prospect—no good!"

If Hughes hadn't pulled the possum out of his shirt and diverted attention by getting up and "Ketchy-ketchying" the little beast, I might not have thought much of what he said. But somehow, Shmoker's crooked tail, Hughes and the possum combined suggested things crooked, deep and cunning—and from that moment, I knew the ground was worth having.

"So long!" Hughes and the possum went off into the night.

"So long! . . . . Hello! what's he going that way for?" I thought.

Instead of turning into Ahlers', Hughes struck out between that pub and Cameron's and disappeared in the dark. This set me to thinking that he was going to hunt up Cameron.

I saw Higgins coming down from the Chink's store and waited for him to pass. O'Regan was with him and Isaac Brown. As soon as they dropped him and went into Ahlers', I tackled the old man.

"Higgins," said I, "Hughes is up to something."

"Good God!" He blurted out as though he had been shot, not waiting to hear what it might be.

"He asked me if I were going out to Buchanan with you to-morrow and I said maybe I would."

"And yer will, won't yer? Look here, sir, I tell you that Mount Buchanan ground is the biggest thing I ever saw—there's millions in it."

"Hughes says there isn't anything."

"My God, what liars some people are! He—why he don't know a bit of quartz from a brickbat. Nothing in it! What's he pegged out all that ground for —seventy-five acres—if there ain't nothing in it?"

"Now, don't go off your head," I said, "I know there's something in it, but Hughes thinks I'm going to peg out and wants to get ahead of me. Now, Higgins, what's to be done? I don't know the track to Buchanan, nor do you—it's pitch dark—the moon won't be up for an hour and I'll bet you drinks they're off to Buchanan the minute they can see."

Higgins cursed his own stupidity in not making me go out to Buchanan before and almost wept. Buchanan had been his pet scheme. He hadn't the money to take up ground, but I had, so he had trusted to me. Now what was to be done?

"Higgins," said I solemnly, "I have a plan."

"My God—what?" cried the old fellow, excitedly.

"You must get drunk, Higgins."

"I—drunk!—Good God, I never did such a thing in my life!"

"Well, Higgins, you must do it now. The fate of Buchanan depends on your getting drunk."

"I can't do it, sir—I can't do it."

"Very well, if you can't you can't."

"My principles, sir!"

"Somebody's got to or we lose Buchanan."

"I've never touched a drop since I came on the field. It would be such a scandal!" The old man paused and thought. "Why must I get drunk?"

"To give me time."

"What for?"

"To save Buchanan."

"For God's sake, how can my getting drunk save Buchanan?"

"Higgins, I know Hughes is going to get ahead of

us. The only way to stop him is to get him drunk. You must do it."

"There's Cameron, too, sir."

"You must fill him up also, Higgins."

"Sir," said the old man solemnly, "I cannot bring myself down so low. I'm a sober, God-fearing, respectable man and if I get drunk, I could never show my face in Maytown again, but, sir, I know a man who would be only too pleased—"

"Higgins, how can you suggest such a thing?"

"Sir, Bob Jenkins would do it like a shot."

"Bob's away out at the Comet."

"Well, then there's Isaac Brown."

This was true. To Isaac a good soak would be a midsummer night's dream. Higgins saw that I hesitated. Before I could stop him, he had called Brown out of Ahlers' bar. "Brown," he said, "Mr. Bellew wents you to get drunk."

"Holy mother—what!"

"Here are a couple of pounds, Brown," I chimed in before he recovered. "I want you to get hold of Cameron and Hughes, start drinking and keep them at it until morning."

"Two pounds! You bet your sweet life! I'll make 'em drunker than lords." Brown, asking no questions, went off in search of Cameron and Hughes, whom he met coming from Wonacott's, in whose paddock they kept their horses hobbled.

"Now, Higgins, who knows the road to Buchanan?" I asked as soon as we had watched Brown manoeuvre his quarry into Ahlers' bar.

"There's no one except Paddy Fahey. He's going out to Mount Madden to-morrow, been making there for months. Buchanan's seven miles beyond, and Paddy's the only man who knows the track."

In a few minutes we stumbled into Paddy's, where a fat girl was playing the "Maiden's Prayer" on an instrument that was once a harmonium. In the old days, a few of "the boys" had celebrated New Year's with its help, and every time drinks were called, they poured a whiskey into its works to give them tone. Now the harmonium groaned and grunted out intermittent noises as though afflicted with chronic asthma.

I was presented to Paddy, and he stopped the "Maiden's Prayer" by introducing me to the fat girl. Then we withdrew with Paddy and drinks to convert him to our needs. Paddy was delighted with me, because I was an Irishman. He was the only man in the field who really knew anything about mining. The Palmer Gold Field comprised about two hundred square miles and, according to Paddy, there was "one damned fool for every square mile." Soon and readily enough, I had him talking about Mount Madden, where he worked.

"Sure, son," he exclaimed, "it's a great show! There's millions of tons of stuff in sight and it all goes about half an ounce. I've been shepherding the ground for over a year and none of 'em knows anything about it but me. There's Buchanan beyond it, too—"

"I hear that's good, Paddy," I broke in.

"Good, son? It's a Mount Moyan over again, but them damned fools, Hughes and Cameron, don't know anything about it at all, at all."

"They don't, eh?"

"Holy mother, why they've pegged right away from the lode. It's running to the east'ard and they've gone north."

"The lode goes east, Paddy?"

"It does, son. Why yez can see the foot-wall in the creek and follow it right up the mountain on the other side. That's the ground to take up."

"Who's got it?"

"No one, son."

"Paddy, I want you to peg out the whole of the eastern ground for me."

"Sure I will, son."

"How much do you want for the job?"

"Sure, yer honor, I'll lave that entoirely to yez. It's thirty mile out and thirty mile in, and the divil's own track, and there's the wages and the horses, and there's lavin' me own worruk and—"

"That's all right, Paddy. Name your price and, if I think it's worth it, I'll pay it."

"Cash down, son?"

Paddy had evidently been bitten before. "Cash down, Paddy." I showed him a roll of notes.

"Make it foive pounds, son, and I'll do it."

"Right, Paddy! When will you start?"

"To-morrow morning, son."

"No, Paddy—to-night."

"Holy God, to-night!"

"Now!"

"Now!" Paddy could not get any other word out.

"*Now*, Paddy, and I'll give you five pounds and another five pounds when you've done the job."

"But, son, it's as dark as the mouth of Hell and me horses are down the river."

I counted out five pounds and toyed carelessly with them. Paddy brought his fist down on the table and cried, "By God, I'll do it."

When I saw he meant business, I handed him the five pounds and told him about Cameron and Hughes intending to get ahead of us.

"Them two damn fools! Why, son, they couldn't find the Buchanan track in the dark to save their skins. It's all they can do to get there by daylight, and I know a short cut round by the Limestone track and Sandy Creek that'll cut off an hour and a half at least."

Then I told him of my plan. He was to round up his horses, saddle the one he intended to ride and tie it up in the bush out of sight. He was to bring in another horse already saddled and hitch him to the post outside the pub. If Hughes suspected and was watching, the hitched horse would keep him from starting till daylight. The moon would be up in half an hour. Paddy could get away then on the hidden horse, peg out fifty acres at Buchanan at dawn and be on his way back before the others got out to the ground.''

Paddy roared. Higgins breathed freely, a weight seemed to be lifted from his mind. ''Done it without getting drunk, sir, thank God!''

Paddy grabbed my hand. ''Buchanan's yours, son, unless I fall down on the road and break me neck.''

Paddy slipped away down the hill, and Higgins and I strolled up to Ahlers', where we found Isaac Brown doing his duty manfully. We helped him along a bit, I taking a drink and old Higgins a cigar, then we strolled out of the bar.

Down the road, now brightly lighted up by the moon, stood a boney old roan all saddled and hitched, and known to every one for a hundred miles around as Paddy's ''Derby Winner.'' In the still of the night, we could hear the quick step of a distant horse and presently, the ''splash—splash—splash!'' of the water as it took the ford at the Palmer River.

Higgins chuckled and his wrinkled old face lit up with glee. ''Taking the Limestone track,'' he whispered, ''strikes off for Buchanan at Dog Leg Creek. It's an awful road, no one but Paddy could pick it up after leaving old Limestone. Hughes and his crowd have to go out by the Queen and cross the river way up at the Alexandra, miles further.''

''When will Paddy get there?''

''Daylight.''

''Well, we agreed to meet him at Mount Madden on his way back. I'm going to turn in.''

''So long!'' Old Higgins went off chuckling and muttering to himself. I, myself, was just going into the yard when I saw Cameron lurch out of the bar. Later on, I learned all that happened.

Cameron clung to the door, his drink-sodden eyes with both arms flung wildly about one of the posts. Suddenly, his wandering eye lighted on Paddy's hitched horse. Drawing his hand across his eyes as if he were not sure of what he saw, he looked again. With a curse, he lumbered back to the bar calling to Hughes

Hughes was singing for dear life all he knew of "Ta-ra-ra-boom-de-ay," which after several years down South he had introduced to the Palmer, where the song won instant favor. He was too drunk to pay any attention to Cameron's excited call.

Cameron clung to the door, his dring-sodden eyes glaring wildly at his fuddled partner. "Paddy Fahey—" he began.

"Paddy Fahey be damned!" cried Ahlers, keeper of the rival pub.

"Paddy Fahey!" roared Cameron.

"Shut up! Have another drink!" yelled Isaac Brown.

Cameron staggered across the room and clutched Hughes by the arm. "Paddy Fahey!" he screamed.

Hughes stopped singing with an ill grace. "Well, what the hell about Paddy Fahey?" he snarled.

"Paddy Fahey—Paddy Fahey's horse is saddled and hitched up ready to start somewhere!"

"Well, what the blaze's that got to do with us?" Hughes brooded only over how soon he could break out into song again.

"Yer damn fool! If Paddy ain't going somewhere, what's his horse saddled up for?"

"Well, s'pose he is?" laughed Hughes. "Why yer blistering idiot, he's going to Mount Madden, what do we care?"

"Like the devil he cares a damn about Mound Madden!"

"Oh to hell with Paddy, let's have another drink!" broke in Isaac Brown.

"Right O!" chimed in Ahlers, reaching for the whiskey.

"Ta-ra-ra-boom-de-ay!" began Hughes again. He attempted a *passeul* on his long thin legs that landed him in a heap on the floor.

"Look here!" cried Cameron, standing over him and shaking a fist in his face, "Look here, if you're too bloody drunk to see, I ain't. I saw Higgins and that damned London chap go into Paddy's just after you came up to my humpy."

"Well, what of it?" Hughes looked owlishly up at the big, black-bearded man standing over him.

"That chap's got to windward of us and he's gone and put Paddy on to going out to Buchanan first."

Hughes sprang to his feet.

"Sh! he's turned in long ago," exclaimed Ahlers, "I seed him ven I vent to the missus for the key to get some more vhiskey."

"And old Higgins?"

"He vas turn in too—I see him."

"Well, then, what's the row?" cried Hughes. "If those two's asleep and Paddy ain't gone yet, we're all right."

"But we shan't be in the morning unless someone starts pretty quick."

"Well, who's to go? By God, I'm too drunk to sit a horse," whimpered Hughes.

"Wouldn't make much difference if you were sober," jeered Brown. When Hughes rode out of camp on a horse, the animal generally came back alone. So did Hughes.

Hughes didn't like the joke. He glared at Isaac with his little beady eyes, hesitating whether to go for him or not. "I believe you know something about this business," he muttered.

"Yer damned smart at knowing things, ain't yer?" sneered Brown.

"You started this drinking to-night, by God!" yelled Hughes.

"By God, so he did!" broke in Cameron.

"Well, you never started any drinking since you came into Maytown, yer loafing swine!" retorted Brown.

"Shentlemen, shentlemen, come now, no rows in 'Mine Haus,' else I turn you all oudt," warned Ahlers.

"Turn us out, be damned! Give us another drink. What's the matter with you all, anyway? Come on, what yer going to have?"

Isaac's offer of drinks put an end to the trouble. But Cameron and Hughes took counsel. They secured a couple of black boys. One, they sent up to Kinnear, with a message telling of their suspicions, and asking that their horses be saddled ready to start for Buchanan at a moment's notice. The other boy, they set on watch over Paddy's horse. At the worst, they could start just as soon as Paddy made a move and two men could peg out quicker than one. Agreeing on this, they settled down to drinking again. Soon, they were all rolling about on the floor, speechless and helpless.

But Kinnear was one of those foxey little men with a long thin nose and ferretty eyes that take no chances. He roused Wonacott, they saddled a couple of horses and came down. One glance at their helpless mates and they decided to run no risk but to start for Buchanan at once.

"But what are we going to do with Hughes and Cameron?" asked Wonacott.

"Leave the swine where they are." Kinnear swung up into his saddle and led the way off.

Shortly afterwards, old Ahlers and his wife woke me by dragging Hughes into the little room boarded off next to mine. Hughes was weeping over Mrs. Ahlers, whom he declared was his best friend on earth, and over Ahlers, who was almost as drunk as himself. At last, between weeping and singing snatches of "Ta-ra-ra-Boom-de-ay," he passed out.

Next morning, I was waked by the sound in the next room of Cameron trying to rouse Hughes. He had great difficulty in making any impression upon his fuddled mate. I heard him whisper hoarsely that Paddy's horse was still hitched to the post.

"Horse? What horse?" mumbled Hughes.

"Paddy's, you fool!"

"Who's a fool! What Paddy?"

"Paddy Fahey—he's not gone to Buchanan."

"What the hell's the use of talking to you!" muttered Cameron, leaving Hughes to himself.

"Gone Buchanan—who's gone Buchanan?"

I turned out and unostentatiously prepared for going to Mount Madden, where we had agreed to go and wait for Paddy on his way back. I had my horses run in and saddled, one with the packs and three for riding. I looked to the saddles, wiped down the horses and gave them a feed of Indian corn, at which luxury they whinnied with delight. Old Higgins loaded up the packs with tea, flour, sardines, jam, sugar, boiled beef, bread and condensed milk, enough to last a week. Every one was astir by the time we came from a good breakfast, lighted our pipes, and got into our saddles. Just as we were starting, Hughes came out looking like a piece of chewed string. He straightened up against one of the verandah posts and waved an arm to me in an uncertain sort of way.

"Off to Buchanan?"

"Yes." I nodded to him. "So long!"

"Well, so long! Good luck!"

"Thanks."

"Going to peg out?"

"Perhaps." I wondered if he were too drunk to remember that Kinnear and Wonacott had started out ahead of us in the night, as Higgins had learned and told me.''

''Well, remember what I told you about the eastern ground. 'Tain't worth a damn. So long!''

''I'll have a look at it, anyway. So long!'' We whipped up into line and away started the ''pack'' with us after it.

Cameron was coming out of Wonacott's place on the top of the hill as we clattered by it.

''Buchanan?'' he shouted, with a grin all over his face.

''Yes,'' I yelled back.

''Good luck!'' Over my shoulder, I saw him wave his arm and caught the universal, ''So long!'' as the horses under Higgins and I and the boy settled down into that long, swinging walk Australian horses keep up through the bush for hundreds of miles at a rate of five or six miles an hour.

We went out past the Queen, and prepared to cross the river at the Alexandre, where we picked up the newly made tracks of two horses going in our direction. The boy got down and examined them.

''That's Wonacott's track. I know that off hind shoe. See the nail holes; there's one too many. Bob Jenkins shoed him last Friday.''

Could we be sure they had taken the long trial? If so, Paddy would have reached Buchanan hours ahead of them. ''Whose is the other track?'' I asked.

''Dunno. See it plainer the other side where the ground ain't so sandy. It's some one with shoes anyway. 'Tain't Bob's—'tain't more'n a five-inch shoe.''

We forded the Palmer and picked up the tracks, quite clear in the soft earth on the other side. ''It's Kinnear's little mare,'' said the boy, after looking at the tracks for a minute.

''How d'ye know?''

''Here's a track in the mud where she's sunk in and turned it over lifting her feet out. She's got a brand burned into the hoof. See it? That's Kinnear's. It ain't got the Government mark, the Q and arrow. Kinnear's is the only mare branded on the hoof up here except the Police.''

So we felt tolerably sure that Kinnear and Wonacott had taken the long route and that Paddy must have beaten them to Buchanan barring mischance. We rode along happily and made his camp at Mount Madden about half past two. We put away our stores in the bough-shed, lighted a fire and barely had the billy boiling before we heard a ''cooee.'' Climbing up the bank of the creek was Paddy's horse with Paddy on its bank roaring with laughter.

''Hullo, Paddy,'' I cried, ''how did you get on?''

''Had the toime of me loife, son.''

''Did you peg out?''

''Did I peg out! I did, son. I did that. Sure I got to Buchanan just as day was breaking, paced out the ground, cut me pegs and druv 'em in and all you've got to do now is to put in your application with the Warden.''

''Did you see any one, Paddy?''

''Wait while I tell ye, son.'' Paddy jumped off the horse, cast loose the saddle and gave the horse a spank which sent it down to the creek for a drink. Then, while we ate, he told us all that had happened.

It seemed that after pegging out, Paddy saddled up and was jogging along quietly to camp when suddenly he came face to face with Kinnear and Wonnacott. The two men drew rein and stared blankly at Paddy. According to Paddy they were so surprised that he himself opened up first:

'' 'The top of the mornin,' says Oi.''

'' 'Where the hell have you come from?' says Kinnear.''

'' 'Buchanan,' says Oi.''

'' 'Buchanan!' says both of 'em together.''

'' 'Yes, says Oi.''

" 'Been peggin' out?' asks Wonnacott.''

" 'That's my bizzness,' says Oi.''

" 'It's mine, too,' says he.''

" 'Ho!' says Oi, 'is it? Well then, the best thing ye can do,' says Oi, 'is to go on about your bizzness and I'll go on about moine. Oi guess if yer mane peggin', yer pegs won't interfere wid moine. Oi've just marked off fifty acres to the east of the creek. Ye'll foind me pegs alongside the prospecting claim.' ''

"What 'll they do?" I asked.

"Nothin'—they can't.''

But we had no more than finished eating, when we saw Kinnear and Wonnacott riding rapidly along the track, and they never even hailed us.

"They're up to something," cautioned Higgins. "P'raps they're going to get in first and lodge an application.''

"They can't do that. Oi've pegged out the ground," objected Paddy.

"No one saw you peg it, Paddy.''

The same idea struck us all. The two men would ride in, swear they had pegged and lodge an application ahead of ours. They would be two to one.

Paddy and I dashed for our saddles, rounded up our horses and went off at a canter to pick up the trail, leaving Higgins and the boy to follow with the pack.

"We've got to take the Dog Leg trail, son," Paddy called out to me, "they've gone by the Queen, and it'll save us an hour and a half.''

Nevertheless, we never drew rein until our worn-out horses stopped at the Warden's office. It was five o'clock and he was just about to leave.

"I want to lodge an application, O'Regan," I announced to the clerk acting as Warden until a new one should be appointed.

"All right, you're just in time. Come in!''

We jumped down and made out the necessary forms. I paid the fees and then, O'Regan, Paddy and I all went over the Ahlers' to have a drink.

As we neared the pub, I saw Hughes sitting on the piazza. He looked up at us with a contented smile on his face.

"Been to Buchanan?" he asked.

"No," I answered.

"Thought you were going."

"So I was."

"Ho!"

His over-confidence was too blissful to disturb. I watched him saunter off to Cameron's. We went into the bar and were talking over the day's doings, when the clatter of hoofs brought us all out on the verandah.

Their horses white with dust and sweat, Kinnear and Wonnacott were riding into camp. When they saw us, they almost dropped from their saddles. They came no nearer than Cameron's, where Hughes came out to meet them, his face wide open with glee.

"Well?" he cried.

"You be damned," snapped Wonnacott.

Hughes's jaw dropped. "Why, what's up?" he demanded.

"You drunken fool! You've lost Buchanan, that's what's up!"

Then, they all disappeared into Cameron's, Hughes last and looking as if he feared that his possum too might turn on him.

The Children's Graves

Every one said said Donald was a "damned good chap." He reminded me of the twelve apostles; I say twelve because I couldn't single out *the one* that came to my mind when I first set eyes on him at the Laura. I recognized a face I knew; the face came back to me out of the long, long ago, and I puzzled over it till I hit it. "Judas"! ! Yes! ! I remembered it now—Judas! with the beautiful eyes—not the scowling, evil-faced, thick-set German of the cheap illustrated Bible—but W. G. Wills Judas, out of "Charles I," whom the King describes to the traitor Murray, beginning the lines, if I remember aright.

I saw a picture once, by a great master. Yes, that was Donald, and he ought to have been roaming about the Laura in a toga and halo; but wore instead an old pair of what had once been grey trousers, very patched and ragged round the bottoms—old blucher boots burst out where the little toe of the right foot should have been. I never saw the toe, but I presume it was there—for the sake of argument we will say it was there—and a smile—a soft, undecided sort of smile. He also wore a white cotton coat, or what had once been a white coat, and a faded cabbage-tree hat. Donald, like Judas, had his price, which, with the characteristic of his race, was generally as much as he could get—for Donald kept a store at the Laura, and also the pub, which he dignified by the name of "York Peninsular Hotel."

I never heard Donald laugh but once. He was a solemn man; he'd a high forehead, soft dark eyes, and a patriarchal beard. He laughed once when we all were sitting around the table at "supper," in the back roped space behind the pub, and I describing how coming down from Mayburn with the women, he overtook the coach in which were two old women in their way to Cooktown.

We all camped at Shepherd's Creek, Graham's place (Graham the teamster). Here he kept a large back-roofed slab building also called a hotel (he bought poor MacDowell out just before that worthy dropped down dead), into which we were all glad to turn. Soon after our arrival the rain came down in torrents. The warden was sandwiched in a little partitioned space between the two old women, who slept in one bed together, and Graham's old woman and daughter-in-law, who slept in another just the other side of him. One of the old women was the German wife of the German Accommodation House keeper (another hotel) at Maytown.

The poor warden, dead tired, couldn't get a wink of sleep, for he lay between, and was the recipient of the whispered confidences of the four women. The two old Maytown women discussed and pulled to pieces in the usual feminine way a young woman who recently arrived at Maytown, and created a stir in that almost God-forgotten place. They left the poor girl without a shred to her back or to her reputation, the conversation ending with a parting shot from the German frau, who clinched all matters relating to the new arrival with "Vaal, she stoppit met me at my hause, ven she coom up mit der coach, and I vas zee all vat she haf got, und she may haf dree vite dressis, but she haf no chemeeses, ain't it."

Donald lifted his arm above his head, bringing his fist down with a bang on the table that made everything jump.

"Chemeeses! My God, Chemeeses!" cried Donald and let a roar out of him that startled the dog and set all the parrots, in a huge home-made cage, screeching.

Donald's wife was on a jaunt, at the time, in Cooktown, at the races on her way home from Herberton, where Donald himself had been the previous year.

I never heard Donald laugh since.

This is where Donald's wife comes in: A rather dominant women with a napoleonic nose, and a look in her hair as if she had been down South a bit trying the "fachons." There was a suspicion of "Titian Red" gone wrong about it, and it looked dusty and dull, with dark patches on the temples and back of the neck, where it was brushed up and put in a "bun." There was also in connection with it, an elaborately curled bunch of uniform colored hair that was given the place of an honored guest in the "front." She wasn't a bad sort though, and usually wore loose wrappers of cotton print, somehow suggesting the ladies one sees standing in the doorways of East Lansdale Street, Melbourne, in the vicinity of the Theatre round the corner, and handy to the "pub" and Parliament House.

But I got interested in the woman, for close to my tent were two little graves, which every evening she used to go and visit with her children. The graves were fenced in from the goats; a few dried-up flowers grew on them, and, under the small mounds in the open, solitary bush, lay all that was left of two little children, who had once been hers.

I used to sit and weave romances round her and the solitary graves—forgetting all about the Titian red of her hair—only seeing the good in the woman, and thinking of the broken-hearted mother.

I asked the "Sub's" wife about it all, and the little thin big-eyed woman got quite pathetic, and told me all the sad story, and I went to my camp and dreamed dreams and wrote a couplet about the dead babies.

"Born in the world—to die,
"They knew no mortal strife.
"Their birth a never-ending death—
"That death, the birth of Life."

I thought I would give the verse to the bereaved mother, and so watched for her the following evening to come to the graves. She had only arrived at the "Laura" the day before from the South, where she had been for a change to Herberton, after the stinging heat of the Summer. Now Herberton has an annual "show," which is the event of Northern Queenstown and supplies topics of conversation to the common folk for a year, until it comes around again.

This year Mrs. Donald was looked up to as a wonderful person, for she had been there. The Duke and Duchess of York's visit paled before the home-coming of Mrs. Donald at the "Laura."

The sun dipped in the West, throwing a red glow over the land, but the shadows were all cast from the East, where the stronger light of a great big full moon rose slowly and majestically shining through the crooked-bowed ironbark trees, standing out like cut patterns in cardboard, all painted black. The silver light made the earth mystical, and the air was full of the loud far-off sounding shrillness of myriad insects, that the coming night or sinking sun had wakened. A solitary chirrup-chirrup close to my tent—the soft call of a dove to its mate from the trees in full bloom, whose delicate scent came to me on the gently-moving soft night air—the screech a long way off of a cockatoo—and the distance deadened tinkle of the bells of hobbled horses, were all the sounds to be heard until presently through the long grey grass came the z-z-z-rup—z-z-z-rup of a woman's dress.

I looked towards the sound and saw a figure advancing to the little graves. The moment seemed sacred; it was the unhappy mother; and I took the pipe from my lips and muttered with reverence, *"Fidelium animoe defanctis; per misericordiam Dei requiescat in pace."*

I felt a little choking in my throat; and the tears came up in my eyes while I watched the lonely figure

lean her arm upon the white rails and gaze into space.
I went back to my tent for the verse I had written,
meaning to hand it to the bereaved mother when she
had come to the front of the tent, and saw the still
motionless figure standing at the graves. She had not
moved. I thought I knew what was passing in her
mind. I remembered the heart-ache I had suffered
when one I loved was almost taken from me. I had gone
through the agony of it all—I had suffered—and I
knew how she was suffering now. I could not see
so far away, in the moonlight, but I pictured the hot
tears trickling down the poor pained face—and for
a moment she seemed transformed—she was beautiful.
I had been standing for perhaps a minute watching,
when, between me and the moonlight, I became conscious of a moving object. It was all in white—almost
ghostlike—and it glided across the Police paddock in
the soft, yielding, unsounding sand, so silently it
seemed almost unreal. I looked steadily and recognized the thin frail figure of the "Sub's" wife. She
glided on and on—past the rough turnstile in the wire
fence of the paddock, and into the long grass, and
towards the solitary figure at the graves. It was a
solemn moment. These two devoted women—in the
solitary bush— a thousand miles from any city—the
one sorrowing, the other, in her womanly way, coming
out into the night to comfort her.

And the two stood in the soft, silver light, alone!
The moon shone gloriously—the silence had grown intense—for the birds were roosting, and the insects
dumb, and the horse bells silent.

God was over all!

Suddenly the stillness was broken. A rather harsh
voice mingled in exclamations of delight with a little
soft one:

"Well, I declare! I didn't know you were back."

"I've had the time of my life. Herberton was
simply great. And you know Emma's not going to

marry Tom; but—she's engaged to another chap."

"No! You don't say."

"Yes, she is. She's going to marry the one they call the 'greasy bounder at the Bank.'"

Then they drifted into "gussets" and "placquets," and "the sleeves ain't worn full any more now" was the last I heard as I turned into my tent, tore up the verse I held in my hand, and, lighting my pipe with it, I strolled over to Donald's pub and told him the "chemise" story over again—at which he was just going to roar, but stopped suddenly, and looked through the open door towards the graves of his little ones. Then we heard the "square-faced" and a half-drunken digger from Ebayoolah start singing on the verandah outside:

"She was h-all—me—fancee—pinted 'er."

"Ho! 'hi never shall forgit!"

" Ho—"

I put down the glass.

"So long, Donald."

"So long! Chemeeses! Lordy! Lordy! cheemeses! Brings back old times! I ain't seen a chemees since last Herb—"

I didn't hear the last of Donald's sentence. I often wondered whether Mrs. Donald did. I passed her with a "Good-night," afterwards, from the shanty door—for Donald never smiled again that I saw.

GOD KNOWS

At the rooms of some artists who formed a colony in the Avenue Frochot, I once knew a young girl of about 18 or 19 years of age—a rare type. She was the forewoman in a millinery department of a large and fashionable store. Every Sunday at an early hour she hurried to her artistic friends in the Avenue Frochot. She entered their quarters as if they were her own, not caring what the people who were there might think, simply saying:

"If I am in the way, send me off."

She was allowed to "circulate," to lounge, to look, at her own free will, to smoke, to sleep, to talk, to sing, to leave when the spirit moved her. A creature of impulse, of natural common sense, having learned nothing for learning's sake, she had acquired in her free life all she knew, which amounted to some knowledge of the piano, some solfege, Italian and English. She read all the printed matter she found, and remembered all she read. I had forgotten to say she was pretty (and it did not detract from her) pretty, very pretty, with a renaissance cameo profile, hair naturally waving, teeth so white, so even, so immaculate that she was made to laugh just to show her teeth. The strangest of all was, that no one ever doubted her perfect womanliness. After staying two or three hours, she would rise, put on her shawl and bonnet (without looking in the glass, so innate was her sense of adjustment); they were always rightly placed, and she would, disappearing, say: "I go to inflict myself elsewhere."

Her departure was as little noticed as had been her arrival.

She was a familiar voice to us, a being, an interest. She said all she thought, listened to her own instinctive feelings, and expressed ideas of nature. We named her Folly. We did not know how she first came to the colony, and no one remembered not having seen her there.

On my return from quite a long journey, I inquired from one of the members of our colony about her. "I've not seen her for months. It is an age since she has been here. She must be dead."

Nothing more was said or thought of her. Artists are careless fellows, we must admit, and women make a sorry mistake to love them.

One morning about the beginning of May, 1855, I was walking through the grand Avenue of Neuilly. I was going to breakfast at the Porte Maillot. I say this for the curious. I had been working steadily for days, and felt the need of giving myself the relaxation of a morning stroll and a country frolic, to establish an equilibrium between the spirit and the flesh, as Zabier de Maistre would say. As I neared the top of the fortifications, I saw the people, particularly the men, walking in an opposite direction from the one I was taking, stop and turn. Some were laughing, others were making that little sound of the lips which is a call for dogs, cats and other animals, and continuing on their way with a sneering air. What silliness!

After quickening my step, I saw quite in the middle of the road, a white kid, jumping, caracoling, by times stopping, running back and forth with the gawky activity natural to young quarupeds when they first feel the earth under their feet, particularly noticeable in the goat kind.

Twenty feet in front of the kid, whose neck had a blue ribbon around it, to which was attached a bell, stood a young women, dressed in a white striped marsailles, made in the picturesque Louis XV style, her face shaded by a large straw hat trimmed with natural flowers. In those days now gone, women still wore hats to protect from the sun. The dress alone of the young woman indicated her indifference to surroundings. She seemed unaware of any attention she was exciting among the passers, and stooping to the level of the object she wanted, called, in the gentlest voice of reproach: "Come on, you little fool!"

There are certain conventional traditions, which do not please me. They hamper men at every turn in their most natural, and often noblest impulses. "This or that is not done," is a despotic phrase, invented by no one knows who, but obeyed unversally, no one knows why. There are hundreds of insignificant prejudices which could be abolished in three days, of which everybody complains, and nobody resists. One of them is this: in the public thoroughfares you cannot go to the aid of a person in a ridiculous situation, without running the risk of becoming ridiculous yourself. It is incredible that in France we should need the opinion of others to be natural ourselves. Often a man or a woman, even a pretty woman, is seen in an embarrassing position and could be extricated by one word, which nobody will speak, or a gesture which no one will make, because they are in the open street. If finally some good Samaritan decides to go to the rescue and relieve the predicament, he turns pale or blushes, almost appeals for approval, then hurries away as soon as possible.

The kid was unwary, and I could easily take him in my arms and carry him to his mistress. It was very simple to do. Why had nobody done it before?

I was thanked with a beautiful courtesy, as I bowed and was about to retire, when with a glance at the young woman, I exclaimed; "Why, is it you?"

To this involuntary remark she ungrammatically replied, "Yes, it is me."

"I had not recognized you."

"I knew you at once."

"Why then did you thank you as if I were a stranger?"

"I did not know whether you cared to recognize me in the street."

"Are you crazy?"

"That is what you all used to call me."

"Where do you live now?"

"At No. 27. I have been to my mother, she lives at No. 8. And you?"

"Me? I am going to Gillette's to breakfast."

"Alone?"

"Yes."

"Come and breakfast with me."

"Thank you; suppose you breakfast with me."

"Just as you wish, I am glad to go, only I must take my kid home."

"Do you like kids?"

"This one was given to me. I take him everywhere, but he's not trained to follow me. See how pretty he it."

And drawing him to her, she showed me his little pink snout, and kissed it as she would a child's rosy lips. She told me then why she was seen no more among the artists. Some one did not wish her to go; he had not confidence in her, had hidden her at Neuilly after having made her leave her work. She lived on her income, spent her days in reading, practicing her music, walking out and playing piquet with her mother. She showed me her apartment on the ground floor with a garden at the back, the plants all nibbled by the kid that she would not shut up.

Three rooms composed her apartment; two were furnished, the parlor bare awaiting the generosity of the somebody who seemed to be in no hurry to furnish it. He was rich, but not extravagantly lavish; prodigality was not among his vices. His family lived at Sevres, his business lived in Paris, he had found a halfway house at Neuilly convenient when he went from Paris to Sevres, and when he returned from Auteuil to Paris. He divided his daily trips, and by this happy combination, met half way in his journeys, youth and love.

Six months after the day on which I found my Esmeralda, the family of the mysterious "he" changed their residence, and went to live at St. Denis. Neuilly was no longer on his road, he ceased stopping there. The parlor was never furnished. The girl was forgotten. No recrimination, complaint, nor revenge was feared from her.

She came to see me and told me these circumstances. I had not seen her since the day I gave her breakfast at Gillette's. She asked my advice. I urged her to return to the store she had left if she could get back her former position.

"I have lost the habit of work," she said in an indefinable way, full of regret and apprehension, "but I will try."

"And the kid?"

"I had him, he's a goat now."

A year after, I was stopped by a blockade of carriages on the corner of Rue Royale. Among the many equipages I saw an open carriage drawn by a pair of magnificent bay horses, admirably groomed. The coachman had trouble in checking them. In the caleche filled with flowers, silk, laces, sat a woman whose eyes were fixed on vacancy, her absent-minded air indicating her unconcern at being there or anywhere. It was she again. The carriage grazed the sidewalk where I stood. I imitated the bleating of a goat; she turned. Recognizing me, she blushed, and hid her face in her two hands with a pretty affected movement of shame, her eyes peeping through her fingers. She seemed to say, "I am naughty, but it's not my fault, forgive, and acknowledge that I look pretty."

My answer was a salutation that might express—
"I congratulate you."

She was about to speak, when the carriage moved
on. Truly she was adorable, under a little rice straw
bonnet trimmed with cherry ribbons. Luxury became
her marvelously.

That evening I received the following note: "I
must talk with you. I long to see you; you will not
come to me; I dare not present myself at your door.
What is to be done?"

I went to the address she indicated. She occupied
all of a hotel in one of the streets parallel to the
Champs Elysees. Tapestries, Venetian chandeliers,
Florentine frames, porcelains of Sevres, Dresden,
Japan, inlaid furniture, Etageres, Jardiniers, mantel
ornaments of the time of Louis XVI,—any one can
imagine it all,—beautiful drawings by Vidal and de
Beaumont, pictures of Isabey and d'Voillemot.

I asked no questions, she made no explanations.
After she had given me a seat, I said:

"What have you to tell me now?"

"Nothing, I wanted to see you."

"Why."

"Just to see you. You bring back pleasant remin-
iscences."

"Are you not happy?"

"I deserve a better fate, I assure you."

She wept, then dried her eyes in a three-hundred
francs handkerchief. We heard the bell ring, a little
maid appeared, and spoke a few words of English to
her mistress, who answered readily in the same tongue.
The maid went out, came back in five minutes, spoke
again and was answered. She repeated this performance five or six times while I was in the parlor.

"Perhaps I'm intruding," and I rose to leave.

"No, stay," she said, "those are my creditors."

I learned that her life was one of confusion, luxury
and debts. She spoke again—"How badly I have fol-

lowed your first advice. Tell me again what to do, all the same.''

"Do you own more than you owe?"

"Oh! yes!"

"Then sell, pay, buy a kid, and return to Neuilly."

"That would be a pity. This is all so pretty."

"Be reasonable, or don't ask advice."

"You are right. I promise——" she paused.

"I owe you a breakfast. When shall it be?"

"Any day you name, but it must be at Neuilly."

"I will be there before another month, on my honor."

"Honor?"

"Yes, an honest girl's honor. May I be hung if I'm not one at the bottom of my heart."

She stayed nevertheless in her fine apartment.

Two years rolled on. She was celebrated for her beauty, her wit, her lavish expenditures, her extravagances of every kind in the eccentric world where she figured.

She came to my apartment one morning, and began abruptly: "Don't tell me all that you think of me. I know it as well as you do, and I have come to ask a favor of you."

"What is it?"

"Have you five hundred francs?"

"Yes."

"Do you like Vidal's work?"

"Yes."

"Give me then five hundred francs, I will send you one of Vidal's pictures. A dealer has offered me that sum for it. I would rather you should own it."

"Take the five hundred francs and keep your picture."

"Now that is unkind," she said. "If I had nothing to give for your money, I would say, make me a present of five hundred francs. When all I have is gone, I will probably ask you for your money, until then

let me have my own way. The picture is my por-
trait, that is why I would rather you should have it
than any one else. It is really pretty; it is an Angel
weeping; the idea is mine, it might be called the Angel
of Repentance. Is it agreed?"

"Yes, but I must pay you a thousand francs,—a
Vidal is worth all of that."

"Honorable people are so queer! So suspicious of
love, they like to make others feel they are free from
all obligation to them and have nothing in common with
them. Put aside five hundred francs. I promise you
to come some day and get them. There, does that
please your pride, are your scruples satisfied?"

"You are then entirely————"

"Ruined! Yes, I am. I have missed my vocation,
the down fall has come. I have been selling and selling,
and yet I cannot stop all the holes."

"What will you do?"

"Do?" She hesitated.

"I will try to live quietly. You will give me then
your advice for the third time?"

"You never follow my suggestion."

"Reproaches? Is this your discount?"

She took the five hundred francs and left. One
hour later I had the drawing by Vidal.

About three years ago, I received the following
note, "I will be at your door tomorrow morning at
nine. Try and see me alone, and give me a whole hour
of your precious time. Important business."

She came on foot. She was rather pale, and a little
thinner, dressed in black; her shoes were not immaculate, her gloves worn at the finger ends. She was no
longer pretty, but beautiful, misfortune gave gravity to
her form and features. Sorrow has the faculty of de-
grading or ennobling the countenance and the manners.
She has lived as reckless an episode as a women can,
her sufferings were the natural sequence, yet she
elicited sympathy. She bore her changed condition

with nobility and courage, without shame, without defiance. What a strange being! Reason had passed through that brain, once open to every breezy influence, and closed the doors again behind all thoughtlessness. She still possessed the charms of her faultless teeth, her ineffable smile, her fresh, sweet, now subdued voice. She saw the impression her dress made upon me.

My clothes have this advantage—they speak for me and relieve me from all explanation. This is the question before me now; in the midst of the errors, and follies, and wickedness of my past life—they have been very many—I have become truly attached to a brave fellow who tried to extricate me from it all. It ruined him; he has no longer father nor mother. He is the Count ———. All he has today is an allowance of eighteen hundred francs from an old uncle, who will no longer see him; he is a consumptive, unable to work. I am two years older than he is, but he wants to marry me, to be certain that I will not leave him. With his title he could marry fortune and family. I have urged him to do so, but he will not. He believes he must die soon and has asked me to stay with him to the last; he loves me; I, too, love him, but as a child; it seems to me that I could be his mother. We are to be married; he insists that it is all settled. When we are married how can we live on eighteen hundred francs? We will not have another cent. He will do whatever I say. Advise me.''

"Go to the country, the real country, and live there. In the first place the open air will be good for your invalid, everything will be cheaper, nobody will know your past life. You can rent a thatched cottage, you will have a peasant cook, you can wear wooden shoes, if necessary, and work a little kitchen garden; in fact, live like peasants, you will none the less be the Count and Countess ———. Don't seek acquaintance, rather avoid them, and you will little by little make for yourselves an interesting position. Your life will be ordinary, the most ordinary existence, but you will have work, respect, rest, and oblivion.''

''You are right,'' she said, and pressed my hand with gratitude. ''I feel that I can do as you say; give me my five hundred francs; they are for my mother, who will go to some institution.'' She kissed me, and I heard nothing more from or of her.

Last summer, in the month of August, I was alone in Paris on business. The weather was admirable. The fancy took me one Saturday to join some friends at G———. To do so I had to take the train for Varennes Saint-Hilaire; there I could hire a carriage and drive to G———. It seemed a little journey; I preferred taking a carriage in Paris and making the trip comfortably all the way in the open air to enjoy the beautiful cool night rather than two hours in a closed train, as I had done a few days before. I made a bargain with the driver for a remise, who assured me that he knew the road. We started at six o'clock. The man went astray in the different roads and crossings we met, and had to ask his way when we reached C———. He was told he had almost turned his back on G———, and would have a drive of nearly an hour and a half more. He declared he would go no further unless he was paid twice the fare agreed. I sent him about his business and went in search of another conveyance.

It was harvest time. The horses had been in the field all the day and would be again the next. Impossible to harness any kind of animal for gold or silver. C——— is not a village, it is only a hamlet. The night had come on; I would have to, unless I slept there, which was not inviting, walk to Varennes Saint-Hilaire, where I would be obliged to take my former combination. It was half-past nine o'clock. I asked my way to Varennes, and, taking up my cour-

age with my two legs, I ventured into a large avenue
of poplars that had been indicated as the road to follow. About the middle of the avenue, which was very
dark, I passed a woman dressed in black, who, after
crossing me, called to me by my name. I turned, and
went straight to her, wondering who could know me
and recognize me at that hour in this village, under
those high poplars. It needed a cat's eyes or a woman's
to do so. It was the new countess.

"What are you doing here?"

"I am on my way to my home, returning from Paris,
where I have been shopping."

"Do you live at C———?"

"Did you not advise me to go to the country?
This, I can assure you, is the real country."

"Then you did follow my advice?"

Every word of it."

"And you find yourself the better for it?"

"Wonderfully. I am perfectly happy. And how
glad I am to see you again."

"Why did you not write me this news?"

"To trouble you again with myself and my
affairs?"

"Your husband?"

"Is as well as possible."

"And your health?"

"Have you matches?"

"Yes."

"Light one, and look at me."

By this improvised light I saw she was fresh and
rosy; she looked only twenty years old.

"How are you? and how do you like our country?"
she continued.

I related my story.

"I will find you a conveyance," she said. "Everybody loves me here. If these people will not let you
have one I will go to the Mayor or the Doctor for
theirs; they are my friends; these bundles are their

commissions. Come with me, only I must go first to my husband; he expects me by this train, and would be uneasy if he did not see me. Do you wish me to introduce him to you?"

"No, I am rather hurried."

"Just as you like, but he's a fine fellow, grateful to you for your advice to me. He had been accustomed to luxury; he loved me, and might have been weak; if we had remained in Paris who knows what follies we would have committed."

During this conversation we were still looking for the conveyance. She entered freely into the houses where I would never have thought of going; everywhere she was welcomed and well received; she knew all the peasant women, their fathers, their children.

"How are you, good mother? I've come to ask a favor of you."

"Anything to please you, dear Countess; sit down." And everybody rose to give her a seat.

As she sat and told my dilemma I was an interested observer of her. Any one would have mistaken her for a country-bred lady, brought up in the free and frank ways of the open-air life, friendly and superior at the same time. What a rapid, perfect and complete change! All she had on could not have cost more than thirty-five or forty francs, but how neat, how sweet, smelling of well-ordered shelves and drawers.

Everywhere the horses had been in use, and we found difficulty; not an animal could be budged before the morning. At last a butcher, in consideration of a good round sum, and to please my little Countess, would drive me on his cart, the one he used for delivery to the customers of the neighboring chateaux. Three leagues from Paris, this is what may happen any day. It was now eleven o'clock at night, the houses were all closed, the moon had risen, the night was fine, the black outlines of the trees seemed sketched on the pearly transparency of the horizon, the depths of the valley could not be seen for the fog, a sure sign of approaching autumn.

We walked on together, waiting for the butcher boy, who was in no haste to return. She told me how her new life delighted her, and asked for news of the Avenue Prochot, and that part of Paris which she no longer visited, even when she went there once a year in a third-class car. She talked of the newest plays, of the latest books. She read all the criticisms in the papers left her. Suddenly she said, "Bye the bye, have you eaten?"

"No."

"You must be hungry?"

"Yes, if there is an inn about here, while waiting for the cart—"

"Every place is closed, but as you will not come to my house, shall I go and get you a piece of bread, a slice of ham and a half bottle of wine? Will that be sufficient?"

"Certainly, but—"

"Wait here for me; I will be back at once."

She disappeared through the shadows of the houses; she ran like a girl of fifteen. I followed in the same direction, to spare her as much as I could of the walk back. She reappeared at the end of ten minutes, bringing my meal in a small basket, such as children use to carry their provisions for the day at school. She took from the basket a small loaf of bread cut in two, a slice of ham in the middle; the bread was stale, the ham dry and very salty. Truly it was not good; I would not tell her so, but gnawed with my teeth, not without repeated effort, into the enormous sandwich, while she poured out wine. About the middle of my meal I had enough. I drank one swallow of the wine, and did not know how to acknowledge without wounding her that my hunger was gone; I feared she would guess why. Half of the bread I still held in my hand.

"Well," said she, "why don't you eat?"

"When the hour for eating is passed one has no appetite. Must I eat it all?" I asked.

"No, indeed."

"Then I throw this away?"

"No, no," she said, laughing, "give it to me," and with an involuntary movement she seized my arm. "This is my dinner," and she bit with her white teeth into the coarse morsel.

THE BLACKBIRD

If Paul Dane were alive now he would be called a "bounder"—probably with good strong double-barreled prefixes to it; but what the sharks left of him is floating about amongst the coral beds somewhere in the New Britain group of islands.

It was long ago.

There were two women: one of the two was Paul Dane's wife, the other wasn't.

Women are queer about men, especially about "bounders"; I dare say you have noticed that. I remember an awfully pretty woman once who had the pick of Melbourne to choose from, but she bolted with a cock-eyed Yankee "drummer," and went barmaiding eventually at Spiers and Ponds in Piccadilly. That was in the early seventies; then she died.

I could tell you of lots of other cases where the "bounders" got the best of it, but they have nothing to do with Paul Dane, so maybe I'll tell you some other time, or perhaps I won't.

There was nothing extraordinary in my first meeting with Dane. I was loafing around Darling harbor watching the ships loading wool for home. I had been roaming over the colonies for some years, and hoped I might pick up a billet round the wharves; but my luck was out and so was my money. I had not even the price of a screw of tobacco on me.

A little tops'l schooner at one of the wharves attracted me; she looked so smart, with taut spars and such a clean entrance and run I could not help standing watching her.

She was a vessel of about a hundred and fifty tons, with a lot of room between decks, where a couple of men were stowing away cases of "Yankee notions";

bales of Manchester goods and cheap German cutlery
filled up her lower hold. I noticed particularly how
beautifully clean below she was, all newly lime-washed;
on deck, although alongside the wharf, she was as
clean as the proverbial new pin.

To a sailor there is something fascinating about the
lines of a pretty vessel, and the little schooner was as
neat a model, for a trader, as one could wish to see.

Seated aft on the cabin top a man was smoking—a
dark-haired, swarthy man—powerfully built, .with
sleeves rolled up over a pair of muscular arms clasped
round his left knee, which was drawn up almost under
his chin. The other leg hung down over the cabin top,
and I could not see it, as I was on the port side and he
sat on the starboard. I knew he wasn't the mate
(mates don't have time to loll around and smoke), so
I supposed he was the captain.

A fringe of black hair around his face made him
pretty ugly, and he had little black, beady eyes that
seemed to glitter, and didn't add to his beauty. It
was the captain; I learned afterwards that his name
was Dane—Paul Dane. He had the reputation of being
one of the smartest traders in the South Seas—which
is saying a good deal for his capacities, both in business
and by way of seamanship.

There was no steam there amongst the islands;
Burns, Philp & Co. had not swallowed the trade, and
good pickings were to be got by smart men who could
keep their vessels off the coral reefs and knew their
way about. Admiralty charts in those days weren't
of any use at all amongst the islands. The best paying
trade, in fact the chief one, was "blackbirding." Now
blackbirding in the South Seas isn't the innocent
amusement of our school days. In plain English it
means stealing natives from the Islands and "contract-
ing" them for labor.

The government has stopped it all now, but in those
times the trade had full swing, and Paul Dane was the

smartest man at it. He had been very successful, made money, bought his own schooner, married quite a pretty little woman, "Promwooloomooloo," who wasn't very particular, not more so than most of her "lady friends" in that district, that is to say.

Shipping clerks and agents used to give him the time of day as they passed on the quay. Altogether Paul Dane was quite "somebody" along the water front of Sydney; amongst the Islands, he was a "terror."

I stood and looked at him, and he, puffing away at his pipe, squinted at me. I was rather a likely lad in those days, and as for sailoring—my heart was in it. From the hour I first put foot on board the old "Conway" in the Mersey, and in spite of many successes in other walks of life, will remain true to the sea till the day it stops beating. There is no life like the sea— none harder, none more thankless, none more precarious—but none so fascinating. I know lots of men who understand what I mean, and can say it better than I can; you may read all about it in their books (and the best sea books are those written by sailors), then you will know, too—and believe me, it is something worth knowing.

I think sailors get nearer to God than people ashore; I mean the real God, without all the trimmings and extras that fence him around on land; we haven't any churches and few parsons at sea.

I remember one old skipper I was with in a large passenger ship being worried by three different parsons in the second class, all different denominations, as to which should read the service on Sunday in the saloon. Each stood out for his own particular creed, and the "old man" at last lost his patience—and roared out: "I'll not have a second-class parson praising God in my first-class saloon, dam'me; gentlemen, I'll read the prayers myself!" And he did. We were under the Union Jack, and so the "old man" rolled out as best

he could the service of the Church of England. It may
or may not be the best in the world, but it is the one
sailors are used to, and they don't care for new-fangled
notions as a rule, whether they have to do with ships
or God.

I was not thinking all these things while I watched
the captain. I was wondering if he wanted a hand—a
wonder soon brought up with a round turn by that
worthy himself.

"Looking for a ship?" cried he.

"Yes," said I.

"Come aboard, then!"

The brawny arms unclasped; the left leg unbent to
its full length; he took the pipe from his mouth, knock-
ing the ashes over the side, gave a grunt and rose to
his full height, about five feet ten.

I scrambled down the ladder which served for a
gang-plank on to the schooner's deck, walked to where
he stood and touched my cap. "I'm Captain Dane,"
said he; "this is my schooner. Going away tomorrow.
If you want a berth I'll sign you on for six months—
wages of the port—bring you back to Sydney."

"I've a mate's certificate, sir," I answered.

"Don't want any mates; only carry one, got him."
This he said indicating a man at the hatchway who
was superintending the taking in of cargo.

"Where are you bound, capt'n?" I asked.

"South Sea Islands."

"Right. I'll go, sir!"

"Meet me at the shipping office at noon tomorrow;
bring your dunnage on board; we cast off early next
morning. If this wind holds we'll get clear of the
heads and make an offing by noon. Want any money?"

"Well—yes, sir!"

"Right; I'll give you a month's advance when you
sign, and here's five bob to clinch the bargain."

I took the five shillings and felt like a millionaire.

"Paul!" Rather a sweet-toned voice came up from the schooner's cabin.

"Coming—my dear."

"Breakfast!" cried the voice. I smelt it—not the voice but the bacon.

Captain Dane turned aft, and as he went down the companion looked my way and said:

"No larks now! You'll come—sure?"

"Sure, sir," said I.

"So long!" and he disappeared.

I climbed the ladder, took a hurried survey of the schooner, and walked away to break my five bob with a good square meal and a pint of beer. By Jove I wanted them—badly.

I was in high spirits.

Having been third mate of a big ship, I never dreamt of having to go before the mast. But that didn't bother me so much, and my thoughts ran helter-skelter till I got dreaming of blue seas and skies—bright coral reefs—fairy-like islands clad with tropical trees—dusky men and women familiar to me in pictures, and a thousand wonders, that, to my imagination, seemed the most desirable things to have seen and known on earth. Isn't youth gorgeous!

A youngster just going to sea from the old "Conway" writes to me now and then; he is crazy about the sea as I was at his age (as I am now!), all eager anticipation to see the sights I have seen, to go where I have been. I shall have a "real good time," as our Yankee cousins say, when that boy comes home from his first voyage and we get together and yarn about it all.

Looking back on life—all the follies of it—all the tragedies—the ups and downs—and the ins and outs—the pleasures and pains—I wonder if I had to live over again whether I would change any of it! We all say we would!

"If I could only start at twenty with the experience I have now.''' a man said in my hearing the other day.

"What an insufferable prig you'd be," replied the other.

I suppose we all should be "insufferable prigs" under those conditions.

Bah! what is the use of youth if we are all to be wise before our time! Of what use the hot blood—the light heart—and the little-thinking lighter head! It is all very well to speculate on what we should have gained—but just think, for one moment, what we should have lost! Think of a sturdy young life tempered with the limpness of age! Think of it! Impulse without the "Imp" or the "pulse"! And where the deuce would youth be, especially without the "Imp"!

But heavens! why am I moralizing (or immoralizing perhaps would be the better word) when my pint of beer is losing its head and my square meal getting cold!

Work-a-day, toiling Sydney passed and repassed the little "pub" where I sat overlooking the glorious harbor, but it all meant nothing to me. My mind was centered on the schooner and her captain. I longed for the night to pass and noon tomorrow to come. I longed to go down to the shipping office, sign on, and go aboard.

"Got a ship, sonny?" said the old woman who owned the weatherboard cottage where half a dozen of us pigged together.

She saw me cramming the few things I had into a canvas bag. Poor old soul! she was a real good sort. Why she ever trusted any of us for a penny God only knows; but she did, and I don't think any of us sold her.

There was a story of a man once who had, but, as she said, "he come from furrin parts," and the story didn't end well for the "Dutchman." Everyone who isn't a Dago is a Dutchman at sea, if he doesn't happen to be English or a Yank.

"Yes, mother"—that was her nickname amongst us.

"That's good news, sonny!"

"I've shipped on the schooner bound for the Islands."

"Ho! 'ave yer? Well, I wish yer well of 'er, my son."

"Why, mother; what's wrong with her?"

"Ho! there ain't nothin' wrong with the schooner, my son."

With what then, mother?"

"Well, they do say that Paul Dane knows 'is was about them h'islands—and 'as got a wife as knows 'er way about Wooloomooloo; but 'e don't take 'er along, they do say."

"Well, that's his affair mother, not mine—is it?"

"No—it ain't your'n, sonny. It ain't your'n—for sure!"

Mother hobbled way about her work muttering, and for a moment I thought of the smell of bacon and the pretty voice from the schooner's cuddy calling Captain Dane to breakfast.

In my heart I hoped the captain's wife was not going to sea with us. I sailed once in a ship with a captain's wife aboard; she was not only wife, but captain too! That ship was a regular hell. I don't know how it was managed, but she got every one on board quarreling. Men seem to get along together all right until a woman comes among them; then it all goes wrong. Yet women are nice enough things as they go. I can't account for it. Noon came at last. My appointment was kept at the shipping office—I signed on —took a "month's advance," carried my bag down to the schooner, stored it away for'rd in the little fo'c'sle —lit my pipe and went ashore again with orders to be aboard ready to heave out from the wharf at daylight. The mate gave me the orders. I noticed him—his face struck me by its frankness and almost feminine beauty.

I noticed, too, that he spoke with a slight accent, which I afterwards found was Scandinavian.

Every one called him "Mr. Chris," his full name, I believe, was Christian Christiansen.

Poor Chris! We became great friends. He's dead, too! How they all seem to die but me! I suppose there is a "little cherub" with an eye on me somewhere "up aloft." But I cannot help thinking there are a lot of good men gone before their proper time—or anyway long before their job was half done.

We were all fond of Chris on board the schooner— all but the captain—for somehow Mr. Chris fell in love with the captain's wife, and that's a great mistake on board ship—or on shore either if it comes to that—at least they say so. I don't think the captain knew it— not really—but anyway there was no cordiality between the two men. We had trouble on board the schooner, though it did not begin with Mr. Chris, but with the captain's wife and another girl they called the "Blackbird"—her name really was "Loalia."

Nearly all the names amongst the Islands are soft-sounding and beautiful. I often wonder people don't use them for their children instead of "Harriet," "Susan," or the common or garden "Jane." Jane! Great Scott! say it over to yourself twice out loud and listen!

Loalia had been caught on a former voyage by the skipper before he married his Wooloomooloo wife. She was enticed to the schooner's side by a tempting red shawl, took the bait, but instead of being sold for labor, Captain Dane installed her as his wife pro-tem, and established her on one of the islands in the New Britain group, where a child was born to her and there were no missionaries.

So Loalia was happy.

She was a beauty, passionate—fond of Paul, but, like her kind, jealous and revengeful.

That's how things stood when I joined the schooner, though I did not know this until after we had reached New Britain.

Well, we warped out, and as there was a fair slant of wind down the harbor the old man didn't bother about a tug, but sheeted home his topsail, set all the fore and aft canvas, and stood for the heads. As we passed through we could see that the clouds low down were banking up in the southeast, so we stood well out from the land, and that night got what we expected, eased our booms forward, canted the yards a little to starboard and stood to the northward with a pretty breeze and a gentle sea on our quarter. It was beautiful weather, with a clear moon almost at the full, and the schooner made good way with everything up aloft "asleep."

I had the deck, and was leaning over the weather rail forward, yarning with a young fellow who had been picked by Mr. Chris along with myself to serve in his watch. Between the puffs at his pipe he was telling me about the "last voyage"—for he had sailed in the schooner before.

"Old man's got his wife aboard this time."

"So I see," I replied, noticing at the same time that he smiled curiously.

"Well—there'll be fun."

"How?" I asked.

"Wait till we get to New Britain."

"What is there up there?"

"Oh—not much—only he's got another of 'em up in the Islands."

"Another what?"

"Why, another Missus."

"Another wife!"

"Well, there ain't any missionaries up there—and there wasn't any fuss or sing-song over it—but she's his missus up there right enough."

"Is that so!"

"Right o'! and there's a kid, too."

"Well! What's he want to take this one up there for then?"

"I dunno—some game he's got, you take your colonial oath!"

Our conversation broke off as four bells struck, and I lay aft to relieve the wheel. From where I stood, the weather side of the wheel, I could see down into the schooner's cuddy, and I noticed that there was a large cabin on each side of the companion ladder, and beyond that the saloon. I supposed these after rooms were the captain's. A light in the little saloon—under the skylight—lit up the place sufficiently to make all clear down below. I saw the port cabin door open, and the captain's wife in a loose flowing white wrapper come. into the saloon—go to the swinging tray and pour out some water from the carafe that stood there surrounded with glasses.

Mr. Chris heard the click of the glasses, and looked down the skylight. Then a strange thing happened.

Mr. Chris was just going to speak to the woman, when she hastily put her finger to her lips as if to command silence—and her eyes glanced quickly at the starboard cabin door. I wondered what it meant. Had they met before? Of course they must have done so—for I had seen her on board—or rather heard her voice the day I agreed to ship and had the conversation with Captain Dane.

My curiosity was awakened, and I watched. Mr. Chris stood looking down the skylight with a smile on his face. The woman "blew" him a kiss with her hand, and then returned abruptly into the cabin, and I heard the click of the handle as she closed the door. Mr. Chris seemed unable to tear himself away, and it wasn't until I struck eight bells that he roused himself, gave a glance aloft—looked all round the horizon—and then stood leaning over the rail gazing to windward.

"Heave the log," he cried out, and the two other hands in the watch lay aft and hove it before the skipper came up to relieve the deck—for Mr. Chris was an "only mate."

"Seven knots, sir," replied the man with the log.

"Seven knots," replied Mr. Chris.

The wheel was relieved. I saw the captain come up the companion. He and Mr. Chris spoke a few words together, and then the mate went below. I turned in wondering!

We worked easily up the coast for the next few days, up inside the Great Barrier reef—through the lovely scenery of the Whitsunday passage—in and out amongst the islands, and along the gloriously beautiful Queensland coast, until finally we rounded Cape Tribulation, and stood in for Cooktown, where we were to call and fill up with water and fresh provisions before proceeding on our voyage.

The road down to the little wharf where we lay dwindled off into a narrow track that wandered away amongst the tropical vegetation around the base of the mountain that formed the southern boundary of the harbor.

Captain Dane had been on deck most of the time, coming up amongst the Islands, and turned in early for a good rest before tackling the rest of the passage north, which is the most difficult navigation inside the reef. We were to sail next day, and he made up his mind to get all the sleep he could now.

His wife in the cool of the evening went for a stroll ashore. Mr. Chris thought he would like to stretch his legs, so after seeing everything cleared up he went over the side, and I, feeling the same way, followed soon after.

There was little to interest me in Cooktown after I had taken a look at the stone marking the supposed spot where Captain Cook hove down the Endeavour, after running her on to one of the sunken reefs off the mouth of the harbor; and, passing two or three open-doored grog shops full of noisy niggers, I wandered back to the schooner, but before boarding her followed the track I had seen in the daylight trending round Mount Cook. The moon was bright, and the view over the bay—the distant ranges on the other side—the entrance to the Endeavour river and Cooktown itself, circled by the range that follows the entire coast line of Queensland—made an enchanting picture.

I was lying on a great boulder of stone to which I climbed, had lit my pipe and was enjoying the beautiful view, when I heard voices approaching from beyond me, and presently, along the path below, I saw a man and a woman advancing slowly. To my amazement I recognized the voice of the man. It was that of Mr. Chris. Who was the woman, though! As they drew near I saw and recognized the captain's wife.

I didn't quite know what to do—whether to make my presence known to them or not. I did not wish to embarrass them, so I lay still on the top of the rock which overhung the path. On they came, talking very earnestly.

"It's no use, Chris, talking like that. I know you love me—loved me long before I ever met him. Can't you be content? I wouldn't marry you, with only a coasting mate's pay—now, could I? You men are so unreasonable."

"You make me mad, woman. I don't know what I'm doing sometimes. I feel I could kill him."

"Ha! ha! you talk like a great big baby, Chris. They'd hang you, Chris, and you wouldn't have me after all. And I'd be a widow—and the schooner and all would be mine. That would be fine, wouldn't it?"

"You don't love him, then?" I could hear the strain in the mate's voice from where I was.

"Love him? Don't be so idiotic, Chris. I had to look out for myself, and he was willing to marry me—most men wouldn't do it."

"I would. By God! I would!"

"Ah!—you say so now—"

"I said so before—"

"Oh! what's the use, Chris? You can't now, so there's an end. Be sensible. I'm going on board again. Come on."

They passed on. I thought to myself, there was a nice little comedy—or tragedy—going on aboard the schooner. But there, it wasn't my picnic; so I knocked the ashes out of my pipe, jumped down off the rock, and strolled quietly and slowly back to the schooner. When I got aboard all was silent, but I noticed the light in the mate's room was not yet out.

Next day, after taking in stores and water, we let go from the wharf about noon, and getting a good slant of wind, stood out to sea and headed north. Captain Dane headed for Lizard Island, and then through one of the breaks in the Great Barrier reef, with which he seemed quite familiar, and instead of coming our way through the coral we soon found ourselves breasting the broad roll of the Pacific, which thundered behind us as it broke with terrific force and grandeur on the barrier. With glorious weather and a fair wind we stood to the northeast, and made an uneventful passage amongst the islands of those seas that make up the great fairyland of the Far East.

No one who has not seen the South Pacific can realize the beauty of it from reading books. So I will not attempt in my little way to describe those southern glories. To me every hour of daylight was a joy, though I own the anxiety of keeping clear of the sunken coral at night was intense. By day one hand was always aloft looking out for the coral, which could be easily detected by the apparent change of color of the water into pale green where it shallowed. But Captain Dane and Mr. Chris seemed to know every reef and exactly where it was, and the schooner never touched a bit of coral all the way.

We were to anchor first in the New Britain Group, and stop over night, ship a quantity of copra, and then proceed to the Ellice group, "blackbirding." In the second dog watch, just before it got dark one evening, the lookout hailed the deck with the welcome cry, "Land on!"

It was the island we were bound for, and from aloft could be seen, as a thin dark line just above the horizon that looked no bigger than a ship's "biscuit."

It was almost calm. The schooner forging ahead slowly, pushed along almost by the send of the swell and the weight of her canvas as it flapped forward, rather than by any real wind there was. Captain Dane took the bearings of the land, and that night we drifted quietly towards it, daylight finding us about five miles off the shore, which shone in the sun against a background of dark tropical vegetation and great palm trees.

I was at the wheel, and I could not help noticing that the captain got fidgety as we neared the island. His wife was lying in a chair under the temporary awning we had rigged up for her—looking towards the island as we neared it.

"Oh! I can see a lot of canoes!—and people!" she said.

"Fishing!" muttered the skipper.

"There's one little canoe with only one fisher in it— oh, a long way nearer to us than the others."

"Man or woman?" asked the captain.

"How stupid you are? How can I tell at this distance? They all look alike."

Dane took the glasses from his wife—a bit roughly, I thought—and raised them to his eyes. He looked steadily, and long—and then holding the glasses out to his wife to take—without looking at her—walked forward a little and stood with his back to her, gazing up aloft.

"What do you make out?" she asked.

"Woman."

"You've got good eyes."

"I know what to look for."

"What?"

"Men—got nothing on—women wear a bit of a grass girdle."

"Oh!" said the wife. "Is that all?"

" 'Bout all."

Then there was silence for a while.

"The woman is paddling the little canoe towards us," she said presently, with the glasses up again.

"Is she?"

Dane didn't seem interested.

"Yes! She's waving a red rag of some sort."

"The devil!" said Dane, and then turning suddenly to his wife he said, "I want to talk to you a minute down below."

He did not wait to see if she followed him down the companion.

The woman rose wonderingly, placed the glasses in her chair and followed. I noticed Mr. Chris, who was on watch, edged up near the skylight. I don't say he was listening, but it looked that way, though all the time he kept his eyes up aloft, as if he was watching the sails. As there wasn't any wind it didn't seem a necessary thing to do.

I heard voices down in the captain's cabin. They seemed angry—there was no mistake about the words which sounded shrilly even through the bulkhead. "You blackguard!"

Then all was quiet. The captain came out of the cabin, and locked the door after him.

"Let me out!" screamed the voice from within. "Let me out, will you?"

"No, I won't. It's no use making a d——d fuss about it. Keep quiet!"

Then he came up on deck and spoke to the mate.

"Look here, Mr. Christian, I don't want to lose any time in this damned place—you understand? Get everything on board as quickly as you can and get away again."

"Afraid we shan't get any wind, sir, just yet," answered the mate.

"Damn the wind! There never was any damned wind when you want it here. We must work her in through the reef the best way we can. If we can't do anything else we must tow her."

"Aye, aye, sir!" And the mate went forward and helped clear away the boat, which was hoisted over the side and passed aft so she would tow astern. The little canoe was slowly nearing us, but was yet a good distance away. I saw a thin black line on the water astern of us, and presently a puff of wind ruffled the sea and the schooner began to fill and gather away. The woman in the canoe waved her red rag and shouted, but the schooner stood on and swept passed her quite close—and I noticed there was a little piccaninny in the bottom of the canoe amongst a lot of bananas, yams, and a dead pig.

Dane waved his hand to the woman, and then turned all his attention to the schooner, which he piloted through the opening in the reef and brought to anchor a few hundred yards from the shore in perfectly still water, so clear that you could easily see the seaweed and the white sand of the bottom.

"Man the boat, Mr. Christian!" called out the captain.

"Three hands lay aft there!"

"Don't allow a soul aboard, d'ye hear?"

"Aye, aye, sir!" Then turning to me the mate said, "That'll do the wheel! That'll do the wheel, sir," and I walked forward.

As I passed along the alley-way, a hand came out of one of the cabin windows and caught me by the leg. "Has the captain gone ashore?"

I was so surprised I scarcely knew what to do, but stammered out "Yes'm." I heard the captain's wife mutter, "Curse him!" as I passed, and then I walked forward.

One event followed quickly on another. First, when we had been anchored about half an hour, the little canoe we had passed at sea came in through the reef and made straight for the schooner. As it shot alongside the woman made fast to the main chains and prepared to spring on board. She was an extremely handsome specimen of the native islander, and almost as clear-skinned as a Samoan girl. In the boat with her sat the little child, which clearly was not a full-blooded native.

The mate stopped the girl from coming on board, and she was evidently furious. She kept calling "Captain, Captain!" and Mr. Chris pointed to the shore, where the captain's boat could be seen hauled up on the beach. The woman's face lit up with joy, and she turned to climb down into the canoe again. As she did so, however, her eyes became fixed on one of the windows of the cabin, and she pointed at it and turned eagerly to the mate. Following the indication of her arm, he looked and saw the captain's wife gazing fixedly at the woman.

"What woman's that?" she asked of the mate. "What woman's that? Can't you answer?"

"I don't know, M'm," answered Mr. Chris.

"You lie, you lie!" screamed Mrs. Dane, from the cabin. "You know well enough. Let me out of this! Do you hear? Let me out!"

"The captain is ashore, m'm; he has taken the key with him."

The native woman still hung to the side, staring at Mrs. Dane. At length an idea seemed to strike her, and she jumped down into the canoe, and, picking up the child, held it high above her head and yelled out, "Captain! Captain!"

Then dropping down, she placed the child safely in the bottom of the canoe, and, seizing the paddle, made her way with vigorous strokes to the shore.

"Now the fat's in the fire!" It was the same lad spoke who had told me of the captain's native wife the night we left Sydney.

"There'll be the devil to pay you see," he continued.

And he was right; there was the devil to pay before morning.

We found afterwards that the captain's wife had taken a bayonet out of the stand of arms in the after-cabin and wrenched the lock off the door. She came up on deck in a towering rage and demanded to be put ashore.

Poor Mr. Chris pointed out to her that he could not get the longboat out, the only one left, and that however much as he wished to please her he could not do what she wanted.

She seized the glasses, and sat down in her chair watching the shore. It so chanced that the woman with the canoe had just reached the beach, where the captain stood in a group of natives, evidently bargaining with them about a lot of copra piled up to be shipped.

The native woman snatched up the child and rushed with him to the captain, throwing her arms about him. He looked for a moment towards the schooner, and then taking up the child marched off into the undergrowth, which on all these islands comes almost down to the water's edge.

The captain's wife lowered the glasses, stood up rigidly for a moment, and then crossing to Mr. Chris, she hissed at him—

"Chris, if you don't revenge me on that man—you need never speak to me again."

"Oh! for God's sake—"

"Remember—Never! never!! so help me, God; I mean it!"

Towards evening the boat came back, and several large canoes plied back and forth from the shore bringing copra to the schooner. Our own boat took our water-kegs and filled up, returning several times to the shore until our tank and water butts on deck were full.

Mrs. Dane made no attempt to go ashore, nor (that I saw) did she speak again to Mr. Chris, who was hurrying about the decks for the rest of the day.

Towards evening the glass began to fall, and a low bank of dark clouds appeared along the horizon. Mr. Chris looked at it several times, and seemed very uneasy. At last he sent word to the captain by the water-boat, drawing his attention to the change, and got word back to haul the schooner outside the reef and have everything ready for sea.

"I'm not going below tonight," Mrs. Dane said to the mate, after she had watched us haul out, and the anchor was down.

It was stiflingly hot, and the atmosphere seemed leaden and thick. "I'll have my bed brought up on deck under the awning."

"Very well, m'm," said the mate.

It was getting dark rapidly, but as yet there was no sign of the captain. Mrs. Dane went below and changed to a thin white wrapper, and then came on deck and lay down on her mattress and apparently fell asleep— for when at last the captain did come on board she never stirred, nor did she wake with the noise of our getting our boat in over the side.

"You'd better get under weigh and out of this place as soon as you can, Mr. Chris."

"Aye, aye, sir" The mate came forward and we soon had the chain hove short and set our canvas aft. Then we hove up, cabled the anchor and got the jib and staysail on her, but she made no way through the water and hardly steered.

It was my wheel. The captain looked at his sleeping wife, and then stretched himself out in her deck-chair and was soon asleep himself. Mr. Chris stood leaning over the rail just forward of the main rigging, and everything was quite still. The bank of cloud had risen half way up the heavens, but above all was clear and the stars were bright. I could hear the sea astern of us as it broke, but beyond that there was no sound. Every now and then a bright gleam in the water showed where some huge fish in the depth below was chasing its prey. The sea was thick with sharks; we had seen them all round us during the day. I thought once I heard the dip of a paddle, but looking in the direction of the sound saw nothing. I don't know how long I had been standing at the wheel; there was not a breath of wind. I suppose I had been leaning over the spokes and dreaming, but suddenly I was called to my senses by an appalling shriek! At the same moment I saw Captain Dane leap to his feet and grapple with a dark figure that stood over his wife with a long native knife raised in the air. It was the native woman I had seen in the canoe.

She flung her arms round the captain with a cry I shall never forget, at the same time throwing the knife from her to the deck. Even in that light I could see the crimson stain of blood upon the white wrapper the captain's wife had on.

Then an awful thing happened. The two swaying figures were wrestling together on the top of the little cabin, when suddenly with a long sigh and wail the wind came tearing along, and her main boom swung over from the port to starboard with a crash, sweeping the captain and the woman over-board into the sea together, as the vessel heeled over gunnel under. There was no time to think. Instinctively, I put the helm down, but she wouldn't come up. I was just in time to shove it hard over to leeward when she luckily paired off and righted.

We lowered our peaks and handed the canvas, and then held her before the wind the best way we could.

Just as the schooner gathered way I heard a horrible shriek, and looking over the quarter saw a smother of phosphorescent light in the blackness of the water and the rushing fins of several sharks which made trails of light similar to the streaks of a match when struck on the wall of a dark room. I knew what that meant, and that the schooner had seen the last of Captain Dane.

The captain's wife lay senseless on the mattress, but she was not dead. The knife had entered her breast high up and evidently gone deep. Mr. Chris got her below—half dragging, half carrying her—and did what he could to stop the bleeding. Once he came up the companion way and said to me—"Will she run before it?"

"I'll keep her as long as I can, sir," I answered,—but the sea was getting up quickly, and I knew she would have to heave-to, sooner or later.

"There's nothing in your way—run her all you can."

"Run her all I can, sir? Aye, aye, sir!"

He went below again.

The seas began to follow too fast, and after about an hour of hard sailing I was afraid they would smother her. I yelled out to Mr. Chris, and he came up on deck looking dazed and ten years older.

Mechanically he set about heaving the schooner to. She was a little beauty to handle, and came up to the wind like a bird, and rode on the gale quietly with a tarpaulin seized in the main rigging and her stern staysail hauled well to windward. I lashed the helm and then set about helping the mate.

"The captain's gone, sir!" I said.

"I know. Yes, I know," his mind seemed wandering. "It's awful—awful!"

"How is she, sir?"

"I don't know. She isn't conscious, but she isn't

dead. How's the barometer?'' It was not low—and had even risen a little.

"Thank God!" muttered the mate. Then after a pause, he put his mouth close to my ear and shouted: "I must get south—the nearest doctor's is Cooktown— I must yet south."

Then he seemed to ponder. Presently quite abruptly he bawled out: "You've a mate's ticket, haven't you?"

"Yes, sir," I yelled back.

"Well, you'll have to be mate now—and come aft with your dunnage."

"Aye, aye, sir!" I felt a glow of exultation at being mate even of a little schooner. The gale was short-lived and soon we were staying our course to the southward with a couple of reefs down, and making good way.

I came aft and took up my quarters in the mate's old room, he moving his gear into the skipper's.

Poor Mr. Chris! He nursed that woman as tenderly as anyone could do, watching her night and day. No one but myself knew the secret he kept hidden away as he thought to himself.

We had crawled slowly down, beating against the southeast wind and were well clear of the islands, and standing in for Cook's passage again in the Great Barrier reef. Mrs. Dane asked to be brought on deck, and so we put up an awning and fixed mattresses on top of the house on which we placed her. She was terribly changed. Death was written clearly in her face, which was bloodless, and her voice was scarcely audible. She looked helpless about—and a faint smile flitted over her lips as she recognized me.

"You've come aft—haven't you?" she whispered.

"Yes, m'm."

"That's good!" Then after a little pause—

"I'm captain of the schooner now, you know. She belongs to me."

"Yes, m'm."

"You can stay with Mr. Chris, if you like."

"Thank you, m'm."

"Mr. Chris!" In an instant he was kneeling by her—his eager eyes straining at her face—"where"— she seemed very faint as she spoke—"When—we—get —to Sydney—you'll be captain—I'll make you captain."

Tenderly he took her hand as he spoke to her, "There! Don't think of that now. You must not talk too much. It isn't good for you to talk."

"Chris, Chris!" her voice was very low.

"Well?"

"Can—you—pray—?"

The tears welled up in the poor fellow's eyes, as he looked at her.

"I haven't been a good woman, Chris, *you—know— that*.

The man groaned and buried his head in his hands.

"Chris—there's a God, pray! A salvation army woman came to me once and told me all about Him,— and I laughed. Chris, do you hear? I laughed!"

"I know, dear, I know!" The tears were trickling down the man's face.

"She told me—all would be right—if I repented— and prayed—Chris, I'm—sorry—" She paused and looked into the sky—then slowly and very earnestly repeated the words—"I—*am*—sorry!"

We knelt by her silently. Presently she spoke again. "Chris, can't you—pray? I never learned how. I never knew—how."

He looked helplessly up at me.

I thought of the words of De Profundis, and repeated them gently—"Out of the depths, O Lord, have I cried unto Thee. Lord hear my voice."

A tear rose in each of her eyes as she put her thin white hands together and whispered after me: "Out— of—the—depths,—O, Lord,—have—I—cried—unto— Thee!—What comes next?"

"O Lord, hear my voice!"

"Lord,—hear—my—voice."

The words seemed to die away upon her lips; her hands fell apart upon her lap; her eyes were fixed upon the infinite blue, and a faint smile played about her parted lips. She was dead!

*　　*　　*　　*　　*　　*　　*　　*　　*　　*　　*

Poor Mr. Chris! He felt it frightfully. We buried her quietly at sea next day, and he sobbed his great heart out over her when we finally sewed her up in some nice clean canvas, and took her out on deck. It was all very sorrowful—very pitiful—and a gloom settled down over the schooner.

Chris never got over it. We stood on for Sydney, but before we reached the Barrier reef I could see his mind unhinged. At length it became evident to everyone on board that he was no longer responsible for what he did, and we held a council at which it was determined that I should take command of the schooner. We let him roam about the vessel, which he did in a harmless way; he never seemed to wish to interfere with anything.

One night I heard him sobbing in the cabin which used to be hers, and the words came out to me—"Out of the depths have I cried unto Thee, O Lord; Lord hear my voice."

*　　*　　*　　*　　*　　*　　*　　*　　*　　*　　*

There was yet one more tragedy on the schooner before we reached Sydney Heads.

No one knew how or when it happened, but the next morning Mr. Chris was not on board.

I brought my first command safely into Sydney, where I saw her sold a few weeks later at public auction.

I never went "blackbirding" again.

A Brief Sketch of Mr. Bellew

Kyrle Bellew, famed actor, manager, dramatist and traveler, who had been suffering from pneumonia, died Nov. 2nd, 1911, at 5 o'clock in the morning, in apartments in the Hotel Utah, Salt Lake City.

Frank A. Connor, the actor's dearest friend and for years his inseparable companion, was the only person with him when the end came. Mr. Bellew was stricken with a cold while playing in Denver, though he attributed his indisposition to the altitude, and was apparently much improved when he reached Salt Lake. He played in the opening performance of the local engagement of his comedy, "The Mollusc," at the Salt Lake Theatre Thursday night. When arising Friday morning he did not feel well and returned to his bed. Later in the day he decided that his ailment was la Grippe; a doctor was called. He was compelled to conceI a luncheon engagement with former Gov. Heber M. Wells, who was an old friend and admirer, arranged for Friday noon. As he continued to grow worse, the balance of his local engagement was cancelled on the advice of his physician. From Friday Mr. Bellew's condition continued to grow more alarming, and it was apparent Tuesday afternoon that the end was but a few hours away. He passed away peacefully, seemingly without pain.

A GREAT LOSS TO THE STAGE.

In the ringing down of a final curtain on Kyrle Bellew's career the English-American stage loses one of its most accomplished actors, and one of the most lovable, highly respected men in the profession. His generosity and broad-mindedness were bywords among his friends. While he called himself a rover, victim of impulse, he was none the less an artist. He was a writer of ability and won success as a dramatist. As his own manager several years ago he was successful. He was at all times, in all places a student capable of teaching the brightest, but ever eager to broaden his own intellect.

During his life there were times that the call of travel and adventure was compelling, more powerful than the lure of the footlights, and the success he was achieving in his chosen profession. At such times he would equip his yacht, Moonstone, for a long cruise, and with his friend Frank A. Connor set sail for some distant land. In this way he visited several times practically every country in the world except Russia, and he was planning with keen anticipation the treat he would give himself when this tour was completed by journeying through Russia.

From Rev. J. C. M. Bellew, well known in England and America as a Shakespearian reader, as well as a minister, Kyrle Bellew inherited his talent for the stage. Previous to the Oxford movement in 1869, which resulted in the resignation of Mr. Bellew's father from the Church of England, and in his entrance to the Roman Catholic Church, the minister had wished his son, Harold, to enter the ministry, but Harold preferred the Navy, following in the footsteps of his grandfather, Admiral Kyrle, and joined H. M. S. "Conway" Training Ship at Liverpool. Leaving the navy at the urgent advice of his father, a move of which he ever afterwards spoke regretfully, Kyrle Bellew set out in 1871 for Australia, which ended in an expedition to the new gold diggings at Yugiltar Reefs. For three years he led a roving picturesque existence, sometimes in affluence and oftener in poverty, trying his hand at gold digging, wood cutting, boat building, sign painting and eventually acting. He returned to England on the death of his father in 1875.

In August of that year he made his first appearance
on the English stage as Woodstock, supporting Helen
Barry in Clancarty, a play which was re-written by
his father's own friend, Tom Taylor. His repetition of
Eglinton Roseleaf in the Park Theatre, London, on
Oct. 16th, 1875, led to his engagement to play under
Buckstone's management at the Haymarket, where he
became leading man, and one of the most popular
young actors in London. Except for a short engagement at the Prince of Wales, he remained three years
at the Haymarket, supporting Adelaide Neilson in Anne
Boleyn, Measure for Measure, The Lady of Lyons, and
other plays, and appearing in the original cast of Gilbert's Engaged. Subsequently he joined Henry Irving
at the Lyceum, in 1878, and Marie Lytton's Company
at the Imperial, obtaining a wide command over a
varied repertoire with such actors as Phelps, Farren,
Brough, Vezin, Rider, and Mrs. Sterling. To his indus-
trious study during these years he attributed his knowledge of theatrical technique, which gave him the rank
in the first class of actors. At the Prince of Wales in
1884, he played Prince Philamir, in the Palace of Truth,
Humphrey Goddard, in Breaking a Butterfly, Gilbert
Vaughan in Called Back, and at the Olympic in 1885
he played Hubert Graham in In His Power, and Carlos
Merle in Heartless.

Although Kyrle Bellew visited America in 1882, he
did not appear on the American stage until 1885, when
Lester Wallack engaged him as leading man. Besides
repeating In His Power, and other plays, for which he
was known in England, his repertoire during two sea-
sons at Wallack's included The Rivals, The Busybody,
Hoodman Blind, Valerie, Sophia, Harvest, The School
for Scandal, Harbor Lights, The Dominee's Daughter,
Old Heads and Young Hearts, and the Romance of a
Poor Young Man. This last play ended the career of
the famous Wallack Company.

From 1887 onward Mr. Bellew played alternately in England and America, with extensive tours in Australia, India and other British Colonial possessions. After a short run at the Gayety, London, in Civil War, in 1887, Henry E. Abbey engaged him as leading man for Mrs. James Brown Potter, with whom he played in nearly all parts of the globe where English is understood. This tour is recalled as one of the unique events of the stage, for although other actors have traveled far and wide they have hardly met with such brilliant success.

After the production of his own Hero and Leander, at the Shaftsbury, London, in 1892, and his appearance in The Lights of Home at the Adelphi, he and Mrs. Potter played together again until 1898 in such dramas as Charlotte Corday and Fracillon. After The Jest, at the Criterion in 1898; Robespierre, at the Lyceum in 1899; and the Ghetto, at the Comedy; he spent another year in the Australian gold fields. He returned to the stage in America, however, in 1902, playing A Gentleman of France, Lady of Lyons, Romeo and Juliet, As You Like It, School for Scandal, Raffles, Sacrament of Judas, Chevalier and the Two Orphans, She Stoops to Conquer, Brigadier Gerard, The Marriage of Reason, The Thief, One Performance; with Mrs. George Gould, in the Plaza Hotel in Mrs. Van Vechten's Divorce Dance; the Builder of Bridges, The Scanday, Revival of Raffles, and the Mollusc.

In addition to his success as a romantic actor Mr. Bellew was a successful dramatist, being the author of the English version of Charlotte Corday, Hero and Leander, Yvonne, Iolande, Francillon, and others.

Mr. Bellew held a master's sailing certificate, having graduated from the New York Nautical School. He was a fellow member of the Royal Microscopal Society, the Royal Geographical Society, The Royal London Yacht Club, and a Life Member of the Actors Fund of America.

Harold Kyrle-Money Bellew was born at Prescott, England. His mausoleum is in St. Raymond's Roman Catholic Cemetery, New York.—Salt Lake City Press, Nov. 3, 1911.